LOGIC

AND

LANGUAGE

LOGIC

AND

LANGUAGE

BERNARD F. HUPPÉ

AND

JACK KAMINSKY

HARPUR COLLEGE, STATE UNIVERSITY OF NEW YORK

NEW YORK: ALFRED A. KNOPF

1961

L.C. catalog card number: 56–6938
© Bernard F. Huppé and Jack Kaminsky, 1956

THIS IS A BORZOI BOOK,
PUBLISHED BY ALFRED A. KNOPF, INC.

PUBLISHED 1956; REPRINTED 1957, 1959, 1961

PREFACE

Two QUESTIONS have been of primary importance to human beings: (1) How do we know that what we know is true, and (2) how can we communicate our knowledge to others. In order to answer these questions philosophers, linguists, and scientists have made intensive investigations into the two instruments used to obtain genuine knowledge—logic and language.

This book serves to introduce the student to some of the fundamental principles that underlie the correct use of logic and language. It is concerned with giving the student some understanding of what it means to think "straight" and to communicate clearly. In order to realize this aim most effectively the book is designed to show how logical and linguistic analyses can clarify the most complicated arguments. Thus the student is asked to examine "real" arguments that have been used by famous writers in the humanities, the social sciences, and the natural sciences. In this way it is hoped that this book will avoid the frequent complaint that books on logic deal only with oversimplified arguments and not with the kind of complex and wordy arguments the student usually meets during his four years of college.

Probably only a little "common sense" would be required to show that if it is true that all men are mortal and John is a man then it must be true that John is mortal. Such an argument is not difficult to understand. The words are few and simple. Their meanings are clear. But only on rare occasions does the student find arguments so clearly and simply presented. The great writers in the arts and the sciences present much more involved writing. Their language is more abstract and their ideas more complicated. Yet it is writing of this kind that the student is usually asked to understand and to evaluate. This book is an attempt to present some tools and techniques which will facilitate the analysis and evaluation of the most abstract arguments.

The first part of the book is an investigation of language. Discussion is centered about what language is and how it originates. Special emphasis is given to those characteristics of language that cause confusion and misunderstanding in argument.

The second part of the book presents the rules of logic and some of the techniques of transforming complicated sentences into logical form. Selections from Saint Augustine and Dostoyevsky are used to show how a knowledge of logic can serve to clarify the reasoning involved in difficult and lengthy arguments.

The authors wish to thank the following for their permission to quote material: D. C. Heath & Co., from *How We Think* by John Dewey; Oxford University Press, from *The Works of Aristotle* translated by W. D. Ross; Random House, Inc., from *Crime and Punishment* by Feodor Dostoyevsky; Alfred A. Knopf, Inc., from *The American Language* by H. L. Mencken; the publishers of *Time*, Inc., *This Week Magazine*, *The Binghamton Press*, and the *Technology Review*; Robert L. McManus, Leslie Lieber, and Charles D. Rice.

We are grateful for the many useful suggestions and criticisms made by Professor John Weld and by the members of the Humanities Division at Harpur College. We are also grateful to the staff of Alfred A. Knopf, Inc., especially Tom Bledsoe, whose criticisms and advice were invaluable. To Alice Kaminsky we are indebted for valuable suggestions and practical assistance.

B. F. H.

J. K.

December 1955

CONTENTS

1. *To Think or Not to Think*   3
   - OBSTACLES TO THINKING   5
   - THE MISUSE OF LANGUAGE   10
   - CONCLUSION   16
   - EXERCISES   17

2. *The Mechanism of Language*   42
   - LANGUAGE IS A MEANS OF COMMUNICATION   43
   - LANGUAGE IS A CREATION OF HUMAN SOCIETY   45
   - LANGUAGE IS BUILT UP FROM SOUND UNITS CALLED *Phonemes*   49
   - THE PHONEMES OF HUMAN LANGUAGE ARE NOT COMPARABLE TO THE SOUNDS MADE BY ANIMALS   53
   - WORDS ARE SELECTED SETS OF PHONEMES WHICH HAVE BEEN GIVEN MEANING   55
   - EXERCISES   56

3. *Meaning in Language*   70
   - SEMANTIC MEANING   70
   - SYNTACTIC MEANING   76
   - LANGUAGE HISTORY: SOCIETY AND THE INDIVIDUAL   82
   - EXERCISES   92
   - RECOMMENDED READINGS: LANGUAGE   108

4. *Validity: Deductive Logic*   110
   - ASSOCIATION, DESCRIPTION, AND ARGUMENT   114
   - VALIDITY   115
   - ARGUMENT AND LANGUAGE   116
   - EXERCISES   119

TYPES OF LOGICAL STATEMENTS   120

EXERCISES   123

THE RULES OF DISTRIBUTION   124

SYLLOGISM   125

THE VALIDITY OF OUR UNITED NATIONS ARGUMENT   132

EXERCISES   132

TRANSLATION OF SENTENCES INTO LOGICAL FORM   133

ENTHYMENE   135

SORITES   136

CONCLUSION   138

EXERCISES   142

APPENDIX TO CHAPTER 4: A SYSTEM OF DIAGRAMS   147

RECOMMENDED READINGS   162

5. *Reliability: Inductive Logic*   163

VALIDITY AND RELIABILITY   163

EXERCISES   166

UNRELIABLE GENERALIZATIONS   166

EXERCISES   168

RELIABLE GENERALIZATIONS   169

EXERCISES   175

HYPOTHETICAL GENERALIZATIONS, OR HYPOTHESES   177

EXERCISES   183

GENERAL EXERCISES   186

RECOMMENDED READINGS   194

6. *Avoiding Error*   195

EMOTIONAL ARGUMENT   196

FAULTY REASONING   200

MISUSE OF LANGUAGE   204

EXERCISES   209

Index   *follows page* 216

LOGIC

AND

LANGUAGE

1

TO THINK OR NOT TO THINK

It was a cold night in Korea and a soldier who was on night sentry duty was looking out in the direction of the enemy. There he could see fires started by an earlier bombardment. Suddenly he could no longer see the light. It seemed to have disappeared. Then, just as suddenly, it reappeared. He was perplexed until it dawned on him that men moving between himself and the enemy might have caused the momentary blotting out of the light. He called for flares and machine guns. A night attack was halted before it had begun. The soldier's quick thinking had saved his outfit from being overrun.

Thinking is what this book is chiefly about, and knowing how to think is important for everyone, even though not everyone will be faced with the soldier's dramatic alternative of thinking clearly or dying. Actually the soldier's problem differs from the problems of everyday living only in its extreme urgency. Here is something to note about thinking: that it is not something special, an activity of an intellectual group. John Dewey makes it clear (see Exercise 4) that thinking takes place in solving the simplest of everyday problems, just as it does in solving the most complex ones of science. As Dewey points out, thinking begins *when a problem*—large or small—*is set and defined.*

A simple question—why does an object fall?—stimulated Newton's inquiries. Einstein began his investigation with an

apparently simple query: why is it that a person who drops
an object from a moving train will see it fall in a straight line,
whereas a person standing on the embankment, watching the
train pass, will see the object fall in an arc? These were the
seemingly simple observations that led to Newton's Law of
Gravitation and Einstein's Theory of Relativity. Although
their problems may have been more "intellectual" than those
of the soldier and may have had less urgency about them, these
differences should not obscure an essential underlying similarity.
The problems of Newton and Einstein, the problem of the
soldier, the problems of everyday living were solved, and can
be solved, only by clear thinking.

To think clearly involves *a search for some principle or set
of principles* that will explain a problem. The soldier sought and
found a simple but correct explanation: if the firelight suddenly
disappeared and then reappeared, it was possible that some
object had moved between the observer and the light. Although
Newton and Einstein were forced to devise complicated theories while the soldier had only to find a simple solution,
they were all engaged in much the same activity of problem-
solving. For the essential activity in thinking is the attempt
to solve a problem by finding an explanatory principle. Thus in
mathematics the solution of equations demands an understanding of underlying principles. History involves the attempt to
understand the general principles which explain why certain
events occurred. Even in writing, a problem is solved when a
principle of organization is found which will enable the writer
to set forth his ideas in proper order.

One final step is involved in the complete and successful act
of thought: *the search for proof and tests*. The soldier's theory
was proved when the flares revealed the enemy. Newton's and
Einstein's theories were accepted because they could be constantly checked and rechecked. The mathematician accepts
mathematical law which can be proved to be free of contradic-
tions. Similarly the historian and the teacher of writing, without
any such positive laws to work with, try always to determine
whether historical events and great literature attest to the existence of acceptable general principles.

Thinking, therefore, consists (1) *in defining a problem*, (2) *in devising principles or hypotheses which will offer a solution,* and (3) *in setting up criteria to test whether these hypotheses or principles are satisfactory.* Looked at in this way, thinking can be sharply differentiated from other kinds of mental activity. For example, daydreaming is not thinking. In daydreaming, ideas are not tested for their truth or consistency; instead, ideas are merely associated with one another at random and with no expenditure of effort. But effort is required to find out why one combination of ideas is true and another false. Such analysis demands great care and patience in checking evidence and conclusions.

In a democracy, where each adult is called upon to decide for himself critical questions of his nation's well-being, the power of thought of the individual citizen is a matter of the most serious import. Yet the evidence suggests that our decisions are not always governed by principles of clear and rational thinking. Frequently, instead of seeing a problem to be solved, we look only for results we would like to see and assume hopefully that because we want these results they will happen. As Plato pointed out (see Exercise 1), men are often frightened of seeing the truth (the "sun"). They are more satisfied with illusions and falsehoods (the "shadows").

There are obstacles in the way of the proper employment of the powers of thought. Before much progress can be made in explaining the principles of effective thinking and the responsible use of the powers of thought some initial attention must be given to the *obstacles to clear thinking,* among which are *escapism, relying on the obvious* (*"seeing is believing"*), and *prejudice.* Careful attention must also be given to the *special problems which language presents.*

OBSTACLES TO THINKING

Escapism. To solve problems is not easy, and the solutions frequently are neither obvious nor popular. For example, most people would be content to "explain" that an apple falls because there is nothing to hold up its weight. Anybody can see *that!* But to state that something is "obvious" and needs no explanation is merely to escape from thought.

Many people do indeed try to "escape" problems. Psychologists tell of numerous instances in which human beings construct their own dream worlds in order to escape from harsh realities. Fortunately, most of us do not go to this extreme. But people have the tendency to avoid resolving problems. They feel that "things will straighten out for themselves" or "everything turns out for the best." They avoid problem solving by adopting a fatalistic attitude: "There is nothing that can be done about it. What will be will be." Such views are really harmful in that they nullify any positive step toward the solution of human ills. And of course they are forms of escapism, since they free the human mind from the tedious job of looking for principles and solutions to specific problems.

Escapism is very clearly seen in daydreaming. Even during the most fascinating discussions our minds may wander momentarily to other subjects. Such an occurrence is normal. But very often such daydreaming completely overshadows the attempt to meet, understand, and resolve real difficulties. It is pleasant to be like Thurber's Walter Mitty who went through life dreaming about what he would like to be. But such evasion of the realities of life often results in disaster for the dreamer who cannot cope with pressing problems.

Another form of daydreaming is misleadingly called "wishful thinking." In such so-called thinking the individual is faced with a genuine difficulty, but instead of seeking to resolve it he escapes into a world of make-believe. Sometimes the escape is into the past. He remembers "how good it was in the old days." Sometimes the escape is into the world of the future with its potentially ideal societies in which everything is perfect. And sometimes the escape is into the world after death. Then he speaks about how nothing really matters in this life. In the next world only goodness will prevail. But even though the past may have been wonderful and the future may be perfect and the next world may contain only goodness, such views are escapisms

when they cause us to ignore or trivialize human problems.
They become serious obstacles to thought.

A form of escapism also characterizes the value attached to
action for its own sake. There are always those who ridicule the
need for careful analysis and inquiry. To them professors "live
in an ivory tower" and thinkers are "eggheads." Hitler's followers believed that action was always preferable to thought. Admittedly unapplied thought can sometimes prove to be sterile.
But action is meaningless and dangerous if it is not guided by
thought. Politicians very often resort to name-calling and high-
sounding phrases rather than to reasoned argument. And, unfortunately, such men are often successful. During a discussion
few people ask themselves whether the argument is legitimate.
Such questioning demands a patience and an effort which most
of us do not want to expend; we do not want to "figure it out
for ourselves." We like to escape from thinking into the security of authority. A child often feels secure when he can
believe in the omniscience of his father. Similarly, an adult
often feels secure when someone else can give him immediate,
positive-sounding answers. But all legitimate answers are obtained only after painstaking inquiry. There is no short cut to
thinking.

Seeing Is Believing. Thinking is sometimes confused with
perceiving. We frequently rely on simple observation without
feeling any need to devise means for testing our observations.
Our attitude is exemplified in the words, "Seeing is believing."
But sense impressions can trick and deceive us. The senses made
us believe that the earth is flat and that the sun goes around it.
But the combination of thought and observation informed us
otherwise. Thinking showed that what people believed they
were seeing they were merely *assuming.* Law courts are in constant difficulty because of the conflicting reports of "eyewitnesses." The history of justice is crowded with cases of men
who have been wrongly imprisoned, even executed, on the positive evidence of several honest "eyewitnesses." For this reason,
proper circumstantial evidence, which rests upon well-thought-
out hypotheses, is often more trustworthy than direct evidence

based solely upon what people believed they saw. In fact, we can never be absolutely certain that we really see what we claim to see. We may believe that there is a tree before us, but it can be an illusion. Moreover, we can be mistaken about the name we give it. We may call it a tree because it resembles many other objects which we are accustomed to call tree. But resemblances often lead to false conclusions. From a distance something may resemble a man but turn out to be a monkey. There are certain objects that resemble wood but are really metallic.

Furthermore, so much agreement about what individuals see is really quite amazing when we consider what is involved in the actual process of seeing. Any biology book will show the complicated path that light must travel through the eye before something is actually seen. Any slight change in this path is sufficient to change what is seen. Thus some people are near-sighted, others are farsighted, and to many the world contains only two or three colors. Since people are so different, it is to be expected that they will "see" differently. Fortunately, the differences are not so great that communication is impossible. But it should be apparent that seeing, hearing, smelling, touching, and tasting are not always reliable guides to believing.

However, despite these depreciatory remarks about the five senses, sensations do play an important role in the accumulation of reliable knowledge. Actually, all knowledge begins with the information derived from the senses. But all such information must be employed with the rigorous instruments supplied by logic, mathematics, and scientific experimentation. Houdini, the great magician, was supposed to have urged that people be trained to observe correctly just as they are trained to work at various trades. Correct observation requires a great deal of careful testing and analysis. If an individual who had never studied physics were to walk into a physics laboratory and see a piece of metal floating in air, he would probably be astounded. But to the trained observer who has a knowledge of magnetic fields the occurrence would be regarded differently. The untrained observer might describe the floating metal in the following way: "It was floating there right in the middle of the

room without any support above or below it. It was a fantastic
occurrence!" The trained observer would say: "It was floating
there right in the middle of the room. It was supported by a
magnetic field that held the metal in equilibrium. It was a perfectly natural occurrence!" Science frequently challenges our
interpretation of what we see. In fact, the scientist is usually
concerned with phenomena which cannot be seen directly. Who
has ever seen the atom or the electron or the neutron that
causes the chain reaction in the atom bomb?

Thinking is also often confused with "experience." Men are
constantly saying, "Oh, I didn't have to go to college to learn
that. I learned it through experience." But experience is an
ambiguous concept. Learning through experience has been
interpreted as a form of learning through perceiving. But perception has already been shown to be quite unreliable unless
analysis is applied to it. Does "experience" simply refer to partic-
ipation in such activities as business or traveling? Such participa-
tion does not in itself create thinking human beings, since
some of the most well-traveled individuals are found to have
superficial understanding. Does learning from experience refer
to learning from the observation of similar instances? Thus
someone might say, "Every time I've met one of their race he's
always been a swindler. So I've learned through experience not
to trust them." But as we shall see in Chapter Five, such
generalizations are fallacious. Experience can deceive us into
accepting falsehoods as well as truths. After all, the criminal
also learns from experience, but he extracts from it what the
thinking individual usually rejects. Learning from experience
depends upon the ability to analyze and extract from perception what is essential and significant. But the discovery of
what is essential and significant requires a knowledge of those
principles which will prohibit false conjectures and train us in
the proper use of evidence.

Prejudice. To a large extent our ideas and beliefs are molded
by biases and prejudices of which we may be wholly unconscious but which serve as obstacles to thought. Bacon's *Idols*
(see Exercise 3) lists the major prejudices that prevent the use
of thought. Because of family and friends we tend to believe

some things more readily than others. The citizen of Moscow, USSR, will have different beliefs from the citizen of Moscow, Pennsylvania. Tradition and environment, rather than thought, sometimes play a decisive role in forming people's beliefs.

Of course even the most "enlightened" individual has some beliefs which are based purely on hearsay and tradition. But the prejudiced person is one who neither allows criticisms of his views nor concedes the possibility that such views may be wrong. The fanatic is condemned primarily because even the most contrary evidence cannot shake his beliefs.

One test of prejudice is to see how an individual responds to criticism of beliefs which are very important to him. He may claim to be unprejudiced yet react emotionally, perhaps even violently, if certain personal views are criticized. Another test of prejudice appears in our reactions to concrete situations. We may believe in racial equality, but how do we react to integration in the schools and in the army? We may believe in freedom of worship, but how do we react to agnostics or atheists? We may believe in the great commandment, "Love thy neighbor," but do we tend to overlook injustice if a man is of a different race, color, or creed? How many times have we secretly approved of such prejudiced statements as "America for Americans," "Foreigners should be sent back to where they came from," "Restricted clientele, and whites only"? We can tell how unprejudiced we really are by judging our reactions to specific instances.

THE MISUSE OF LANGUAGE

When misused, language can itself become an obstacle to effective thinking. There is particular danger in this fact because language is so much a part of us that we are not usually aware of the difficulties in the way of its responsible use. For this reason language is treated at considerable length in this book.

Reliance upon prejudice rather than thought is sometimes fairly obvious. For example, a Northerner writing about the Civil War might reveal a different set of attitudes and beliefs than a Southerner writing about the same war. But usually prejudice is not so clearly discernible. Only the most rabid demagogue explicitly states his hatreds and his biases. In most cases prejudice is subtly hidden in language, as in the following descriptions by two reporters:

Reporter A: The President's wife wore a colorful red dress.
Reporter B: The President's wife wore a loud red dress.

Each sentence refers to the same fact. But the use of adjectives such as *loud* and *colorful* shows the reporters' bias and also evokes either favorable or unfavorable reactions. When words can cause such reactions, there is always the risk that our actions will be prompted more by emotions than by thought and facts. Words such as *overweight, fat,* and *pudgy* may all name the same characteristic. But whereas a person might become worried if he were called "overweight" he might become angry if he were called "fat" or "pudgy." A series of words can all refer to the same object or event, but they may also be able to arouse different emotions. For this reason a wrong word can very often be sufficient to induce a mood that is immune to any intellectual argument. In fact, in some societies magical properties are attributed to certain words. Thus among the Karok Indians mention of a dead man's name was extremely dangerous and was punishable by death or payment of a large sum of money.

Nor are such *taboo* words found only in primitive societies. Even the so-called civilized mind avoids the use of certain words. The men who handle our dead are always searching for a name which will disguise what they are doing:

A *mortician* never handles a *corpse;* he prepares a *body* or *patient.* This business is carried on in a *preparation-room* or *operating-room,* and when it is achieved the patient is put into a *casket* and stored in the *reposing-room* or *slumber-room* of a *funeral home.* On the day of the funeral he is moved to the *chapel* therein for the last exorcism, and then hauled to the cemetery in a *funeral-car* or *casket-coach.* The old-time shroud is now a *négligé* or *slumber-shirt* or *slumber-robe,* the mortician's work-truck is an *ambulance*, and the cemetery is fast becoming a *memorial-park*. In the West cemeteries are being supplanted by public mausoleums, which sometimes go under the name of *cloisters, burial-abbies*, etc. (H. L. Mencken, *The American Language*, pp. 287–88.)

There are also taboo words that are referred to as "four-letter" words which have a continuous history in the English language from the earliest times. Although these words appear in print very seldom, they may be heard fairly frequently, except in "polite" society. Such taboo words are illustrated in the following report on their use among college students in Georgia and Tennessee:

> Stedman . . . got such words as *guts, stink*, and *belly*, the last being the most offensive word that these young people could bring themselves to write down and submit to a professor. Hunter and Gaines [had students check] a list of 62 words [which] . . . contained only the milder sort of taboo words. The eight least freely used words in the list are *bitch, puke, whore, bastard, belly, guts, belly-ache*, and *harlot*. Less objectionable are *vomit* (for which the students substitute *throw-up, regurgitate*, or *unswallow*), *breast* (substitutes: *bosom, chest*), *pants, sweat*. (E. H. Sturtevant, *Introduction to Linguistic Science*, p. 126.)

But the emotional quality of language is not limited to taboo or "four-letter" words, for most words do contain some kind of emotional content. Usually the problem of choice in searching for the right word is the problem of selecting the word with the most exact emotional content. Even such an apparently "neutral" word as *shirt* suddenly stirs hidden feelings when it is used in the phrase *Hitler's Brown Shirts*.

The choice of a right word is no easy matter despite the existence of unabridged dictionaries. Writers have been known to spend days and even weeks searching for the "right" word or phrase. Flaubert supposedly spent years writing and rewriting a sentence! Unfortunately, people sometimes believe that if they search long enough they will find the proper word. But actually there is no such thing as "the" word. A great writer may describe a scene in such a way that we are practically a part of it. But his description is not, therefore, the "correct" one. There are an indefinite number of ways of writing and speaking about the same object or event. The difficult problem of the relation of word to thing will be explored in Chapter Three. Here it is important to note merely that word and object do not fit into a neat equation. No *one* word is indispensable in the description of an object. Any object may be described and any idea may be expressed in many different ways. But the words that are used will determine whether an analysis of a given issue will be understood and critically evaluated.

The difficulty of finding words that will not interfere with the thought to be expressed is further complicated by the fact that both spoken and written words are ambiguous. Poor Alice discovered the potential ambiguity of speech in talking to the Red and White Queens:

> Here the Red Queen began again. "Can you answer useful questions?" she asked. "How is bread made?"
>
> "I know that!" Alice cried eagerly. "You take some flour . . ."
>
> "Where do you pick the flower?" the White Queen asked. "In a garden or in the hedges?"
>
> "Well, it isn't picked at all," Alice explained, "it's ground . . ."
>
> "How many acres of ground?" said the White Queen. . . .

The ambiguity of sound has succeeded in barring proper communication between Alice and the two willful queens. Another example of a similar breakdown in communication once appeared in a newspaper report which described how a recruit broke ranks during maneuvers and plunged into the woods at his left, after an officer had shouted, "Bear to the right." The recruit explained, "I'm afraid of bears."

Not only do some words sound alike, but almost every word has several meanings, so that potential misunderstanding constantly threatens to interfere with thought. Consider the various meanings of the word *air:* "As he was taking the air, he whistled an air, but as the air escaped from his lips, he looked up in the air and aired his pleasure, breathing the air with an air of delight." Consider the potential ambiguity in the word *law,* which, on the one hand, signifies a prescription of what people are required to do under penalty, and, on the other hand, signifies a description of a given set of events, for example, the language habits of a specific group.

Legal law prescribes what ought to be; grammatical law merely describes what *is.* Yet the ambiguity of the word *law* may occasion misunderstanding. Thus persons are accused of violating a law of grammar quite as if they had violated a prescriptive law. They are said, for example, to be "wrong" in splitting an infinitive because this is a violation of the laws of good grammar. Yet well-educated speakers of English quite characteristically split infinitives. Grammatical law should faithfully describe this fact of language usage. Nonetheless, people will look guilty when they are "accused" of violating the law against using the split infinitive, though no law, in the prescriptive sense, exists. In like fashion, the English teacher gets used to having new acquaintances remark: "Oh, you're an English teacher. I guess I'd better watch my grammar." Almost universally the English teacher is looked upon as a guardian of the laws of language, as the policeman is looked upon as the guardian of the laws of the land. The ambiguity in the meaning of the word *law* is one of the causes of a confusion which serves as an obstacle to thought, and which may nullify the attempt to give expression to reasoned argument.

An obstruction to thought and communication also appears in the ambiguity that results from faulty sentence structure. Perhaps only someone whose job it is to answer letters from the citizenry can appreciate how widespread is this kind of ambiguity. Here are a few excerpts of letters actually received by official bureaus. They were excerpted, it might be noted, because they happen to be funny, not because they are uncommon.

I can't pay. I got six children. Can you tell me why this is?

Sir, I am forwarding my marriage certificate and my two children. You can see one is a mistake.

You have changed my little girl to a boy. Does that matter?

In accordance with your instructions, I have given birth to twins in the enclosed envelope.

Even though examples of this kind may not seem serious, the ambiguities of language and the possibilities of interpreting words and sentences in more than one way can have serious consequences. The law student knows how important it is to make language say precisely what he wishes it to say. What seems to be tortuous and overcomplicated legal jargon actually results from the difficult attempt to use language so precisely that no confusion can occur. Lawyers have learned from experience that a misplaced connective such as *and* may spell a loss of thousands of dollars in insurance claims. "Loopholes" in the law which have permitted notorious criminals to escape punishment are frequently caused by nothing more than a misplaced modifier.

The improper use of metaphor can cause confusion in thought. In a metaphor the meaning of a word or a phrase is extended to include more than it originally did. Thus the word *ox* usually refers to some kind of strong animal. But the meaning has been extended when we say "Jones is an ox." The extension of meanings can sometimes be used for amusing effects. In certain rare moments men refer to women as "little buttercups" or "sugar pies." Women speak of men as "strong, handsome devils" or "drips."

Metaphor can also have profound and significant effect on events. Thus the phrase *Iron Curtain* in one sense means a curtain made of a certain kind of metal. But when Winston Churchill used this phrase to refer to Russian policy, the words referred to more than simply a metallic object. Churchill's hearers recognized at once that he was not describing a physical thing—an iron curtain—but a foreign policy which would prevent those living inside the Russian orbit from seeing what was happening in the rest of the world, and which would prevent the rest of the world from seeing what was occurring in Russia. The power of the metaphor is that it summarizes and makes possible a positive attitude toward Russia. In so doing it performs its function very well. But the metaphor can at the same time be harmful in that it can arouse too much emotion and be interpreted too loosely. Thus *Iron Curtain* arouses feelings of love or hate, and, at the same time, seems to imply that we can never communicate through such a curtain. Such a response decreases rather than increases the possibility of resolving world problems through peaceful means. Metaphor, with its vagueness and emotional appeal, can serve as an obstacle to thought.

Language is one of mankind's greatest assets. But at the same time, as Aristotle points out (see Exercise 2), like any useful tool, it can be employed carelessly and dangerously. It can serve as the most important means for conveying information but it can also defeat the search for knowledge and the application of thought. And in this atomic age such a defeat can be disastrous. Only at great risk can we avoid the study of thinking and of language.

CONCLUSION

These introductory remarks have served chiefly to indicate that effective thinking is not easy to achieve. The effective thinker must contend against various obstacles to thought. In particular he must be on guard against the tendency of language to hamper not only the proper communication of thought, but even thought itself. He must know something about the *mechanism of language* and about *meaning in language,* so that he may understand how these may interfere with reasoned argument. The next two chapters will treat these two subjects, preparatory to a study of the principles of effective thinking.

1. *"Myth of the Cave," from Plato,* The Republic, *Book VII,* tr. A. D. Lindsay.

"Then after this," I said, "liken our nature in its education and want of education to a condition which I may thus describe. Picture men in an underground cave-dwelling, with a long entrance reaching up towards the light along the whole width of the cave; in this they lie from their childhood, their legs and necks in chains, so that they stay where they are and look only in front of them, as the chain prevents their turning their heads round. Some way off, and higher up a fire is burning behind them, and between the fire and the prisoners is a road on higher ground. Imagine a wall built along this road, like the screen which showmen have in front of the audience, over which they show the puppets."

"I have it," he said.

"Then picture also men carrying along this wall all kinds of articles which overtop it, statues of men and other creatures in stone and wood and other materials; naturally some of the carriers are speaking, others are silent."

"A strange image and strange prisoners," he said.

"They are like ourselves," I answered. "For in the first place do you think that such men would have seen anything of themselves or of each other except the shadows thrown by the fire on the wall of the cave opposite to them?"

"How could they," he said, "if all their life they had been forced to keep their heads motionless?"

"What would they have seen of the things carried along the wall? Would it not be the same?"

"Surely."

"Then if they were able to talk with one another, do you not think that they would suppose what they saw to be the real things?"

"Necessarily."

"Then what if there were in their prison an echo from the opposite wall? When any one of those passing by spoke, do you

imagine that they could help thinking that the voice came from
the shadow passing before them?"

"No, certainly not," he said.

"Then most assuredly," I said, "the only truth that such men
would conceive would be the shadows of those manufactured
articles?"

"That is quite inevitable," he said.

"Then consider," I said, "the manner of their release from
their bonds and the cure of their folly, supposing that they
attained their natural destiny in some such way as this. Let us
suppose one of them released, and forced suddenly to stand up
and turn his head, and walk and look towards the light. Let us
suppose also that all these actions gave him pain, and that he
was too dazed to see the objects whose shadows he had been
watching before. What do you think he would say if he were
told by someone that before he had been seeing mere foolish
phantoms, while now he was nearer to being, and was turned to
what in a higher degree is, and was looking more directly at
it? And further, if each of the several figures passing by were
pointed out to him, and he were asked to say what each was, do
you not think that he would be perplexed, and would imagine
that the things he had seen before were truer than those now
pointed out to him?"

"Yes, much truer," he said.

"Then if he were forced to look at the light itself, would not
his eyes ache, and would he not try to escape, and turn back to
things which he could look at, and think that they were really
more distinct than the things shown him?"

"Yes," he said.

"But," I said, "if someone were to drag him out up the steep
and rugged ascent, and did not let go till he had been dragged
up to the light of the sun, would not his forced journey be one
of pain and annoyance; and when he came to the light, would
not his eyes be so full of the glare that he would not be able to
see a single one of the objects we now call true?"

"Certainly, not all at once," he said.

"Yes, I fancy that he would need time before he could see
things in the world above. At first he would most easily see

shadows, then the reflections in water of men and everything else, and, finally, the things themselves. After that he could look at the heavenly bodies and the sky itself by night, turning his eyes to the light of the stars and the moon more easily than to the sun or to the sun's light by day?"

"Surely."

"Then, last of all, I fancy he would be able to look at the sun and observe its nature, not its appearances in water or on alien material, but the very sun itself in its own place?"

"Inevitably," he said.

"And that done, he would then come to infer concerning it that it is the sun which produces the seasons and years, and controls everything in the sphere of the visible, and is in a manner the author of all those things which he and his fellow-prisoners used to see?"

"It is clear that this will be his next conclusion," he said.

"Well, then, if he is reminded of his original abode and its wisdom, and those who were then his fellow-prisoners, do you not think he will pity them and count himself happy in the change?"

"Certainly."

"Now, suppose that those prisoners had had among themselves a system of honours and commendations, that prizes were granted to the man who had the keenest eye for passing objects and the best memory for which usually came first, and which second, and which came together, and who could most cleverly conjecture from this what was likely to come in the future, do you think that our friend would think longingly of those prizes and envy the men whom the prisoners honour and set in authority? Would he not rather feel what Homer describes, and wish earnestly

> To live on earth a swain,
> Or serve a swain for hire,

or suffer anything rather than be so the victim of seeming and live in their way?"

"Yes," he said, "I certainly think that he would endure anything rather than that."

"Then consider this point," I said. "If this man were to descend again and take his seat in his old place, would not his eyes be full of darkness because he had just come out of the sunlight?"

"Most certainly," he said.

"And suppose that he had again to take part with the prisoners there in the old contest of distinguishing between the shadows, while his sight was confused and before his eyes had got steady (and it might take them quite a considerable time to get used to the darkness), would not men laugh at him, and say that having gone up above he had come back with his sight ruined, so that it was not worth while even to try to go up? And do you not think that they would kill him who tried to release them and bear them up, if they could lay hands on him, and slay him?"

"Certainly," he said.

"Now this simile, my dear Glaucon, must be applied in all its parts to what we said before; the sphere revealed by sight being contrasted with the prison dwelling, and the light of the fire therein with the power of the sun. If you will set the upward ascent and the seeing of the things in the upper world with the upward journey of the soul to the intelligible sphere, you will have my surmise; and that is what you are anxious to have. Whether it be actually true, God knows. But this is how it appears to me. In the world of knowledge the Form of the good is perceived last and with difficulty, but when it is seen it must be inferred that it is the cause of all that is right and beautiful in all things, producing in the visible world light and the lord of light, and being itself lord in the intelligible world and the giver of truth and reason, and this Form of the good must be seen by whosoever would act wisely in public or in private."

"I agree with you," he said, "so far as I am capable."

"Come, then," I said, "and agree with me in this also; and don't be surprised that they who have come thus far are unwilling to trouble themselves with mortal affairs, and that their souls are ever eager to dwell above. For this is but natural if the image we have related is true."

"It is," he said.

"Then do you think it at all surprising," I said, "if one who has come from divine visions to human miseries plays a sorry part and appears very ridiculous when, with eyes still confused and before he has got properly used to the darkness that is round him, he is compelled to contend in law courts or elsewhere concerning the shadows of the just or the images which throw those shadows, or to dispute concerning the manner in which those images are conceived by men who have never seen real justice?"

"No, it is anything but surprising," he said.

"Yes," I said, " a sensible man would remember that the eyes may be confused in two ways, and for two reasons—by a change from light to darkness, or from darkness to light. He will consider that the same may happen with the soul, and when he sees a soul in trouble and unable to perceive, he will not laugh without thinking; rather he will examine whether it has come from a brighter light and is dim because it is not accustomed to the darkness, or whether it is on its way from ignorance to greater brightness and is dazzled with the greater brilliance; and so he will count the first happy in its condition and its life, but the second he will pity, and if he please to laugh at it, his laughter will be less ridiculous than that of him who laughs at the soul that has come from the light above."

1) (a) What do the following symbolize: the "cave"? the "chains"? the "images"?
   (b) What is meant by the fact that the chained persons can see only shadows?
   (c) Why do they not realize that they are only shadows? Has this anything to do with "Seeing is believing"?
   (d) What is meant by the philosopher's journey to the sun?

2) What has this selection to do with "obstacles to thought"? What specific section in Chapter 1 is developed here?

3) Assuming that you agree with Plato, what changes in education would you recommend?

2. *"False reasoning,"* *from Aristotle,* De Sophisticis elenchis, tr. W. A. Pickard—Cambridge.

That some reasonings are genuine, while others seem to be so but are not, is evident. This happens with arguments, as also elsewhere, through a certain likeness between the genuine and the sham. For physically some people are in a vigorous condition, while others merely seem to be so by blowing and rigging themselves out as the tribesmen do their victims for sacrifice; and some people are beautiful thanks to their beauty, while others seem to be so, by dint of embellishing themselves. So it is, too, with inanimate things; for of these, too, some are really silver and others gold, while others are not and merely seem to be such to our sense; e.g. things made of litharge and tin seem to be of silver, while those made of yellow metal look golden. In the same way both reasoning and refutation are sometimes genuine, sometimes not, though inexperience may make them appear so: for inexperienced people obtain only, as it were, a distant view of these things. For reasoning rests on certain statements such that they involve necessarily the assertion of something other than what has been stated, through what has been stated: refutation is reasoning involving the contradictory of the given conclusion. Now some of them do not really achieve this, though they seem to do so for a number of reasons; and of these the most prolific and usual domain is the argument that turns upon names only. It is impossible in a discussion to bring in the actual things discussed: we use their names as symbols instead of them; and therefore we suppose that what follows in the names, follows in the things as well, just as people who calculate suppose in regard to their counters. But the two cases (names and things) are not alike. For names are finite and so is the sum-total of formulae, while things are infinite in number. Inevitably, then, the same formulae, and a single name, have a number of meanings. Accordingly just as, in counting, those who are not clever in manipulating their counters are taken in by the experts, in the same way in arguments too those who are not well acquainted with the force of names

misreason both in their own discussions and when they listen
to others. For this reason, then, and for others to be mentioned
later, there exists both reasoning and refutation that is apparent
but not real. Now for some people it is better worth while to
seem to be wise, than to be wise without seeming to be (for
. . . the sophist is one who makes money from an apparent but
unreal wisdom); for them, then, it is clearly essential also to
seem to accomplish the task of a wise man rather than to accomplish it without seeming to do so. To reduce it to a single
point of contrast it is the business of one who knows a thing,
himself to avoid fallacies in the subjects which he knows and to
be able to show up the man who makes them; and of these accomplishments the one depends on the faculty to render an
answer, and the other upon the securing of one. Those, then,
who would be sophists are bound to study the class of arguments
aforesaid: for it is worth their while: for a faculty of this kind
will make a man seem to be wise, and this is the purpose they
happen to have in view.

1) This passage differs from selection 1 in the way it is written. Does it differ in what it says?
2) What is Aristotle's definition of genuine "reasoning"?
Comment.

---

3. *"The Idols of Thought," from Francis Bacon,* Novum Or-
ganum *(condensed and renumbered).*

THE IDOLS

There are four classes of Idols which beset men's minds. To
these for distinction's sake I have assigned names—calling the
first class *Idols of the Tribe*; the second, *Idols of the Cave*; the
third, *Idols of the Market-place*; the fourth, *Idols of the Theatre.* (1) The Idols of the Tribe have their foundation in human nature itself, and in the tribe or race of men. For it is a
false assertion that the sense of man is the measure of things.
On the contrary, all perceptions as well of the sense as of the

mind are according to the measure of the individual and not according to the measure of the universe. And the human understanding is like a false mirror, which, receiving rays irregularly, distorts and discolors the nature of things by mingling its own nature with it.

(2) The Idols of the Cave are the idols of the individual man. For every one (besides the errors common to human nature in general) has a cave or den of his own, which refracts and discolors the light of nature; owing either to his own proper and peculiar nature; or to his education and conversation with others; or to the reading of books, and the authority of those whom he esteems and admires; or to the differences of impressions, accordingly as they take place in a mind preoccupied and predisposed or in a mind indifferent and settled; or the like. So that the spirit of man (according as it is meted out to different individuals) is in fact a thing variable and full of perturbation, and governed as it were by chance. Whence it was well observed by Heraclitus that men look for sciences in their own lesser worlds, and not in the greater or common world.

(3) There are also Idols formed by the intercourse and association of men with each other, which I call Idols of the Market-place, on account of the commerce and consort of men there. For it is by discourse that men associate; and words are imposed according to the apprehension of the vulgar. And therefore the ill and unfit choice of words wonderfully obstructs the understanding. Nor do the definitions or explanations wherewith in some things learned men are wont to guard and defend themselves, by any means set the matter right. But words plainly force and overrule the understanding, and throw all into confusion, and lead men away into numberless empty controversies and idle fancies.

(4) Lastly, there are Idols which have immigrated into men's minds from the various dogmas of philosophies, and also from wrong laws of demonstration. These I call Idols of the Theatre; because in my judgment all the received systems are but so many stage-plays, representing worlds of their own creation after an unreal and scenic fashion. Nor is it only the systems now in vogue, or only of the ancient sects and philoso-

phies, that I speak; for many more plays of the same kind may
yet be composed and in like artificial manner set forth; seeing
that errors the most widely different have nevertheless causes
for the most part alike. Neither again do I mean this only of
entire systems, but also of many principles and axioms in science, which by tradition, credulity, and negligence have come
to be received.

But of these several kinds of Idols I must speak more largely
and exactly, that the understanding may be duly cautioned.

THE IDOLS OF THE TRIBE

(1) The human understanding is of its own nature prone to
suppose the existence of more order and regularity in the world
than it finds. And though there be many things in nature
which are singular and unmatched, yet it devises for them
parallels and conjugates and relatives which do not exist. Hence
the fiction that all celestial bodies move in perfect circles; spirals
and dragons being (except in name) utterly rejected. Hence too
the element of Fire with its orb is brought in, to make up the
square with the other three which the sense perceives. Hence
also the ratio of density of the so-called elements is arbitrarily
fixed at ten to one. And so on of the other dreams. And these
fancies affect not dogmas only, but simple notions also.

(2) The human understanding when it has once adopted an
opinion (either as being the received opinion or as being agree-
able to itself) draws all things else to support and agree with it.
And though there be a greater number and weight of instances
to be found on the other side, yet these it either neglects and
despises, or else by some distinction sets aside and rejects; in
order that by this great and pernicious predetermination the
authority of its former conclusions may remain inviolate. And
therefore it was a good answer that was made by one who when
they showed him hanging in a temple a picture of those who
had paid their vows as having escaped shipwreck, and would
have him say whether he did not now acknowledge the power
of the gods—"Ay," asked he again, "but where are they painted

that were drowned after their vows?" And such is the way of all superstition, whether in astrology, dreams, omens, divine judgments, or the like; wherein men, having a delight in such vanities, mark the events where they are fulfilled, but where they fail, though this happen much oftener, neglect and pass them by. But with far more subtlety does this mischief insinuate itself into philosophy and the sciences; in which the first conclusion colors and brings into conformity with itself all that come after, though far sounder and better. Besides, independently of that delight and vanity which I have described, it is the peculiar and perpetual error of the human intellect to be more moved and excited by affirmatives than by negatives; whereas it ought properly to hold itself indifferently disposed towards both alike. Indeed in the establishment of any true axiom, the negative instance is the more forcible of the two.

(3) The human understanding is moved by those things most which strike and enter the mind simultaneously and suddenly, and so fill the imagination; and then it feigns and supposes all other things to be somehow, though it cannot see how, similar to those few things by which it is surrounded. But for that going to and fro to remote and heterogeneous instances, by which axioms are tried as in the fire, the intellect is altogether slow and unfit, unless it be forced thereto by severe laws and overruling authority.

(4) The human understanding is unquiet; it cannot stop or rest, and still presses onward, but in vain. Therefore it is that we cannot conceive of any end or limit to the world; but always as of necessity it occurs to us that there is something beyond. . . . The human understanding being unable to rest still seeks something prior in the order of nature. And then it is that in struggling towards that which is further off it falls back upon that which is more nigh at hand; namely, on final causes: which have relation clearly to the nature of man rather than to the nature of the universe. . . .

(5) The human understanding is no dry light, but received an infusion from the will and affections; whence proceed sciences which may be called "sciences as one would." For what a man had rather were true he more readily believes. Therefore he

rejects difficult things from impatience of research; sober things, because they narrow hope; the deeper things of nature, from superstition; the light of experience, from arrogance and pride, lest his mind should seem to be occupied with things mean and transitory; things not commonly believed, out of deference to the opinion of the vulgar. Numberless in short are the ways, and sometimes imperceptible, in which the affections color and infect the understanding.

(6) But by far the greatest hindrance and aberration of the human understanding proceeds from the dullness, incompetency, and deceptions of the senses; in that things which strike the sense outweigh things which do not immediately strike it, though they be more important. Hence it is that speculation commonly ceases where sight ceases; insomuch that of things invisible there is little or no observation. . . . For the sense by itself is a thing infirm and erring; neither can instruments for enlarging or sharpening the senses do much; but all the truer kind of interpretation of nature is effected by instances and experiments fit and apposite; wherein the sense decides touching the experiment only, and the experiment touching the point in nature and the thing itself.

(7) The human understanding is of its own nature prone to abstractions and gives a substance and reality to things which are fleeting. But to resolve nature into abstractions is less to our purpose than to dissect her into parts; as did the school of Democritus, which went further into nature than the rest. Matter rather than forms should be the object of our attention, its configurations and changes of configuration, and simple action, and law of action or motion; for forms are figments of the human mind, unless you will call those laws of action forms.

Such then are the idols which I call *Idols of the Tribe*; and which take their rise either from the homogeneity of the substance of the human spirit, or from its preoccupation, or from its narrowness, or from its restless motion, or from an infusion of the affections, or from the incompetency of the senses, or from the mode of impression.

THE IDOLS OF THE CAVE

The *Idols of the Cave* take their rise in the peculiar constitution, mental or bodily, of each individual; and also in education, habit, and accident. Of this kind there is a great number and variety; but I will instance those the pointing out of which contains the most important caution, and which have most effect in disturbing the clearness of the understanding.

(1) Men become attached to certain particular sciences and speculations, either because they fancy themselves the authors and inventors thereof, or because they have bestowed the greatest pains upon them and become most habituated to them. But men of this kind, if they betake themselves to philosophy and contemplations of a general character, distort and color them in obedience to their former fancies; a thing especially to be noticed in Aristotle, who made his natural philosophy a mere bond-servant to his logic, thereby rendering it contentious and well nigh useless.

(2) There is one principal and as it were radical distinction between different minds, in respect of philosophy and the sciences; which is this: that some minds are stronger and apter to mark the differences of things, others to mark their resemblances. The steady and acute mind can fix its contemplations and dwell and fasten on the subtlest distinctions: the lofty and discursive mind recognizes and puts together the finest and most general resemblances. Both kinds, however, easily err in excess, by catching the one at gradations the other at shadows.

(3) There are found some minds given to an extreme admiration of antiquity, others to an extreme love and appetite for novelty; but few so duly tempered that they can hold the mean, neither carping at what has been well laid down by the ancients, nor despising what is well introduced by the moderns. This, however, turns to the great injury of the sciences and philosophy; since these affectations of antiquity and novelty are the humors of partisans rather than judgments; and truth is to be sought for not in the felicity of any age, which is an unstable thing, but in the light of nature and experience, which

is eternal. These factions therefore must be abjured, and care must be taken that the intellect be not hurried by them into assent.

(4) Contemplations of nature and of bodies in their simple form break up and distract the understanding, while contemplations of nature and bodies in their composition and configuration overpower and dissolve the understanding. . . . These kinds of contemplation should therefore be alternated and taken by turns; that so the understanding may be rendered at once penetrating and comprehensive, and the inconveniences above mentioned, with the idols which proceed from them, may be avoided.

Let such then be our provision and contemplative prudence for keeping off and dislodging the *Idols of the Cave*, which grow for the most part either out of the predominance of a favorite subject, or out of an excessive tendency to compare or to distinguish, or out of partiality for particular ages, or out of the largeness or minuteness of the objects contemplated. And generally let every student of nature take this as a rule—that whatever his mind seizes and dwells upon with peculiar satisfaction is to be held in suspicion, and that so much the more care is to be taken in dealing with such questions to keep the understanding even and clear.

THE IDOLS OF THE MARKET-PLACE

But the *Idols of the Market-place* are the most troublesome of all: idols which have crept into the understanding through the alliances of words and names. For men believe that their reason governs words; but it is also true that words react on the understanding; and this it is that has rendered philosophy and the sciences sophistical and inactive. Now words, being commonly framed and applied according to the capacity of the vulgar, follow those lines of division which are most obvious to the vulgar understanding. And whenever an understanding of greater acuteness or more diligent observation would alter those lines to suit the true divisions of nature, words stand in the way and resist the change. Whence it comes to pass that the high and formal discussions of learned men end oftentimes in disputes about words and names; with which (according to the use and wisdom of the mathematicians) it would be more prudent to begin, and so by means of definitions reduce them to order. Yet even definitions cannot cure this evil in dealing with natural and material things; since the definitions themselves consist of words, and those words beget others: so that it is necessary to recur to individual instances, and those in due series and order. . . .

(1) The idols imposed by words on the understanding are of two kinds. They are either names of things which do not exist (for as there are things left unnamed through lack of observation, so likewise are there names which result from fantastic suppositions and to which nothing in reality corresponds), or they are names of things which exist, but yet confused and ill-defined, and hastily and irregularly derived from realities. Of the former kind are Fortune, the Prime Mover, Planetary Orbits, Element of Fire, and like fictions which owe their origin to false and idle theories. And this class of idols is more easily expelled, because to get rid of them it is only necessary that all theories should be steadily rejected and dismissed as obsolete.

(2) But the other class, which springs out of a faulty and unskillful abstraction, is intricate and deeply rooted. Let us take for example such a word as humid. . . . When you come to apply the word—if you take it in one sense, flame is humid; if in another, air is not humid; if in another, fine dust is humid; if in another, glass is humid. So that it is easy to see that the notion is taken by abstraction only from water and common and ordinary liquids, without any due verification.

(3) There are however in words certain degrees of distortion and error. One of the least faulty kinds is that of names of substances, especially of lowest species and well-deduced (for the notion of *chalk* and of *mud* is good, of *earth* bad); a more faulty kind is that of actions, as *to generate, to corrupt, to alter*; the most faulty is of qualities (except such as are the immediate objects of the sense), as *heavy, light, rare, dense*, and

the like. Yet in all these cases some notions are of necessity
a little better than others, in proportion to the greater variety
of subjects that fall within the range of the human sense.

THE IDOLS OF THE THEATRE

But the *Idols of the Theatre* are not innate, nor do they
steal into the understanding secretly, but are plainly impressed
and received into the mind from the play-books of philosophical
systems and the perverted rules of demonstration. . . . *Idols
of the Theatre*, or of Systems, are many, and there can be and
perhaps will be yet many more. For were it not that now for
many ages men's minds have been busied with religion and
theology; and were it not that civil governments, especially
monarchies, have been averse to such novelties, even in matters speculative; so that men labor therein to the peril and
harming of their fortunes—not only unrewarded, but exposed
also to contempt and envy; doubtless there would have arisen
many other philosophical sects like to those which in great
variety flourished once among the Greeks. For as on the phenomena of the heavens many hypotheses may be constructed,
so likewise (and more also) many various dogmas may be set
up and established on the phenomena of philosophy. And in
the plays of this philosophical theatre you may observe the
same thing which is found in the theatre of the poets, that
stories invented for the stage are more compact and elegant,
and more as one would wish them to be, than true stories out
of history.

In general however there is taken for the material of philosophy either a great deal out of a few things, or a very little
out of many things; so that on both sides philosophy is based
on too narrow a foundation of experiment and natural history,
and decides on the authority of too few cases. For the Rational
School of philosophers snatches from experience a variety of
common instances, neither duly ascertained nor diligently examined and weighed, and leaves all the rest to meditation and
agitation of wit.

There is also another class of philosophers, who having bestowed much diligent and careful labor on a few experiments, have thence made bold to educe and construct systems; wresting all other facts in a strange fashion to conformity therewith.

And there is yet a third class, consisting of those who out of faith and veneration mix their philosophy with theology and traditions; among whom the vanity of some has gone so far aside as to seek the origin of sciences among spirits and genii. So that this parent stock of errors—this false philosophy—is of three kinds; the Sophistical, the Empirical, and the Superstitious.

The most conspicuous example of the first class was Aristotle, who corrupted natural philosophy by his logic: fashioning the world out of categories; assigning to the human soul, the noblest of substances, a genus from words of the second intention; doing the business of density and rarity (which is to make bodies of greater or less dimensions, that is, occupy greater or less spaces), by the frigid distinction of act and power; asserting that single bodies have each a single and proper motion, and that if they participate in any other, then this results from an external cause; and imposing countless other arbitrary restrictions on the nature of things; being always more solicitous to provide an answer to the question and affirm something positive in words, than about the inner truth of things. . . . In the physics of Aristotle you hear hardly anything but the words of logic; which in his metaphysics also, under a more imposing name, and more forsooth as a realist than a nominalist, he has handled over again. Nor let any weight be given to the fact, that in his books on animals and his problems, and other of his treatises, there is frequent dealing with experiments. For he had come to his conclusion before; he did not consult experience, as he should have done, in order to the framing of his decisions and axioms; but having first determined the question according to his will, he then resorts to experience, and bending her into conformity with his placets leads her about like a captive in a procession; so that even on this count he is more guilty than his modern followers, the schoolmen, who have abandoned experience altogether.

1) What are the "idols"? Name them and describe each. How are they related to the discussion in Chapter One?
2) What is Bacon's remedy for avoiding the idols?
3) What is the relation of Bacon's idols to Plato's? What basic difference is involved?
4) In the light of the selection from Aristotle, do you find Bacon's dismissal of Aristotle justified? Consider particularly the idols of the market-place in formulating your answer.
5) Bacon makes seven points about the idols of the tribe. What are they? Discuss.
6) What general rule does Bacon give for handling the idols of the cave?
7) Why do the idols of the market-place cause the greatest difficulty?
8) What types of "name" problems does Bacon discuss?
9) What, according to Bacon, are the three types of false philosophy? Discuss.

---

4. *"The Five Steps in Thought," from John Dewey,* How We Think.[1]

In this chapter we shall make an analysis of the process of thinking into its steps or elementary constituents, basing the analysis upon descriptions of a number of extremely simple, but genuine, cases of reflective experience.[2]

(1) "The other day when I was down town on 16th Street a clock caught my eye. I saw that the hands pointed to 12:20. This suggested that I had an engagement at 124th Street, at one o'clock. I reasoned that as it had taken me an hour to come down on a surface car, I should probably be twenty minutes late if I returned the same way. I might save twenty minutes by a subway express. But was there a station near? If not, I might lose more than twenty minutes in looking for one. Then I thought of the elevated, and I saw there was such a line within two blocks. But where was the station? If it were

1 Reprinted by special permission of D C. Heath and Company, Boston.
2 These are taken, almost verbatim [according to Dewey] from the class papers of students.

several blocks above or below the street I was on, I should lose time instead of gaining it. My mind went back to the subway express as quicker than the elevated; furthermore, I remembered that it went nearer than the elevated to the part of 124th Street I wished to reach, so that time would be saved at the end of the journey. I concluded in favor of the subway, and reached my destination by one o'clock."

(2) "Projecting nearly horizontally from the upper deck of the ferryboat on which I daily cross the river, is a long white pole, bearing a gilded ball at its tip. It suggested a flagpole when I first saw it; its color, shape, and gilded ball agreed with this idea, and these reasons seemed to justify me in this belief. But soon difficulties presented themselves. The pole was nearly horizontal, an unusual position for a flagpole; in the next place, there was no pulley, ring, or cord by which to attach a flag; finally, there were elsewhere two vertical staffs from which flags were occasionally flown. It seemed probable that the pole was not there for flag-flying.

"I then tried to imagine all possible purposes of such a pole, and to consider for which of these it was best suited: (a) Possibly it was an ornament. But as all the ferryboats and even the tugboats carried like poles, this hypothesis was rejected. (b) Possibly it was the terminal of a wireless telegraph. But the same considerations made this improbable. Besides, the more natural place for such a terminal would be the highest part of the boat, on top of the pilot house. (c) Its purpose might be to point out the direction in which the boat is moving.

"In support of this conclusion, I discovered that the pole was lower than the pilot house, so that the steersman could easily see it. Moreover, the tip was enough higher than the base, so that, from the pilot's position, it must appear to project far out in front of the boat. Moreover, the pilot being near the front of the boat, he would need some such guide as to its direction. Tugboats would also need poles for such a purpose. This hypothesis was so much more probable than the others that I accepted it. I formed the conclusion that the pole was set up for the purpose of showing the pilot the direction in which the boat pointed, to enable him to steer correctly."

(3) "In washing tumblers in hot soapsuds and placing them mouth downward on a plate, bubbles appeared on the outside of the mouth of the tumblers and then went inside. Why? The presence of bubbles suggests air, which I note must come from inside the tumbler. I see that the soapy water on the plate prevents escape of the air save as it may be caught in bubbles. But why should air leave the tumbler? There was no substance entering to force it out. It must have expanded. It expands by increase of heat or by decrease of pressure, or by both. Could the air have become heated after the tumbler was taken from the hot suds? Clearly not the air that was already entangled in the water. If heated air was the cause, cold air must have entered in transferring the tumblers from the suds to the plate. I test to see if this supposition is true by taking several more tumblers out. Some I shake so as to make sure of entrapping cold air in them. Some I take out holding mouth downward in order to prevent cold air from entering. Bubbles appear on the outside of every one of the former and on none of the latter. I must be right in my inference. Air from the outside must have been expanded by the heat of the tumbler, which explains the appearance of the bubbles on the outside.

"But why do they then go inside? Cold contracts. The tumbler cooled and also the air inside it. Tension was removed, and hence bubbles appeared inside. To be sure of this, I test by placing a cup of ice on the tumbler while the bubbles are still forming outside. They soon reverse."

These three cases have been purposely selected so as to form a series from the more rudimentary to the more complicated cases of reflection. The first illustrates the kind of thinking done by everyone during the day's business, in which neither the data, nor the ways of dealing with them, take one outside the limits of everyday experience. The last furnishes a case in which neither problem nor mode of solution would have been likely to occur except to one with some prior scientific training.

The second case forms a natural transition; its materials lie well within the bounds of everyday, unspecialized experience; but the problem, instead of being directly involved in the person's business, arises indirectly out of his activity, and accordingly appeals to a somewhat theoretic and impartial interest. We shall deal in a later chapter with the evolution of abstract thinking out of that which is relatively practical and direct; here we are concerned only with the common elements found in all the types.

Upon examination, each instance reveals, more or less clearly, five logically distinct steps: (i) a felt difficulty; (ii) its location and definition; (iii) suggestion of possible solution; (iv) development by reasoning of the bearings of the suggestion; (v) further observation and experiment leading to its acceptance or rejection; that is, the conclusion of belief or disbelief.

(1) The first and second steps frequently fuse into one. The difficulty may be felt with sufficient definiteness as to set the mind at once speculating upon its probable solution, or an undefined uneasiness and shock may come first, leading only later to definite attempt to find out what is the matter. Whether the two steps are distinct or blended, there is the factor emphasized in our original account of reflection—*viz.*, the perplexity or problem. In the first of the three cases cited, the difficulty resides in the conflict between conditions at hand and a desired or intended result, between an end and the means for reaching it. The purpose of keeping an engagement at a certain time, and the existing hour taken in connection with the location, are not congruous. The object of thinking is to introduce congruity between the two. The given conditions cannot themselves be altered; time will not go backward nor will the distance between 16th Street and 124th Street shorten itself. The problem is *the discovery of intervening terms which when inserted between the remoter end and the given means will harmonize them with each other.*

In the second case, the difficulty experienced is the incompatibility of a suggested and (temporarily) accepted belief that the pole is a flagpole, with certain other facts. Suppose we symbolize the qualities that suggest *flagpole* by the letters *a*, *b*, *c*;

those that oppose this suggestion by the letters *p, q, r*. There is, of course, nothing inconsistent in the qualities themselves; but in pulling the mind to different and incongruous conclusions they conflict—hence the problem. Here the object is the discovery of some object (O), of which *a, b, c,* and *p, q, r,* may all be appropriate traits—just as, in our first case, it is to discover a course of action which will combine existing conditions and a remoter result in a single whole. The method of solution is also the same: discovery of intermediate qualities (the position of the pilot house, of the pole, the need of an index to the boat's direction) symbolized by *d, g, l, o,* which bind together otherwise incompatible traits.

In the third case, an observer trained to the idea of natural laws or uniformities finds something odd or exceptional in the behavior of the bubbles. The problem is to reduce the apparent anomalies to instances of well-established laws. Here the method of solution is also to seek for intermediary terms which will connect, by regular linkage, the seemingly extraordinary movements of the bubbles with the conditions known to follow from processes supposed to be operative.

(2) As already noted, the first two steps, the feeling of a discrepancy, or difficulty, and the acts of observation that serve to define the character of the difficulty may, in a given instance, telescope together. In cases of striking novelty or unusual perplexity, the difficulty, however, is likely to present itself at first as a shock, as emotional disturbance, as a more or less vague feeling of the unexpected, of something queer, strange, funny, or disconcerting. In such instances, there are necessary observations deliberately calculated to bring to light just what is the trouble, or to make clear the specific character of the problem. In large measure, the existence or non-existence of this step makes the difference between reflection proper, or safeguarded *critical* inference and uncontrolled thinking. Where sufficient pains to locate the difficulty are not taken, suggestions for its resolution must be more or less random. Imagine a doctor called in to prescribe for a patient. The patient tells him some things that are wrong; his experienced eye, at a glance, takes in other signs of a certain disease. But if he permits the sug-

gestion of this special disease to take possession prematurely of his mind, to become an accepted conclusion, his scientific thinking is by that much cut short. A large part of his technique, as a skilled practitioner, is to prevent the acceptance of the first suggestions that arise; even, indeed, to postpone the occurrence of any very definite suggestion till the trouble— the nature of the problem—has been thoroughly explored. In the case of a physician this proceeding is known as diagnosis, but a similar inspection is required in every novel and complicated situation to prevent rushing to a conclusion. The essence of critical thinking is suspended judgment; and the essence of this suspense is inquiry to determine the nature of the problem before proceeding to attempts at its solution. This, more than any other thing, transforms mere inference into tested inference, suggested conclusions into proof.

(3) The third factor is suggestion. The situation in which the perplexity occurs calls up something not present to the senses: the present location, the thought of subway or elevated train; the stick before the eyes, the idea of a flagpole, an ornament, an apparatus for wireless telegraphy; the soap bubbles, the law of expansion of bodies through heat and of their contraction through cold. (a) Suggestion is the very heart of inference; it involves going from what is present to something absent. Hence, it is more or less speculative, adventurous. Since inference goes beyond what is actually present, it involves a leap, a jump, the propriety of which cannot be absolutely warranted in advance, no matter what precautions be taken. Its control is indirect, on the one hand, involving the formation of habits of mind which are at once enterprising and cautious; and on the other hand, involving the selection and arrangement of the particular facts upon perception of which suggestion issues. (b) The suggested conclusion so far as it is not accepted but only tentatively entertained constitutes an idea. Synonyms for this are *supposition, conjecture, guess, hypothesis,* and (in elaborate cases) *theory.* Since suspended belief, or the postponement of a final conclusion pending further evidence, depends partly upon the presence of rival conjectures as to the best course to pursue or the probable explanation to favor, *cultivation of a*

variety of alternative suggestions is an important factor in good thinking.

(4) The process of developing the bearings—or, as they are more technically termed, the *implications*—of any idea with respect to any problem, is termed *reasoning*. As an idea is inferred from given facts, so reasoning sets out from an idea. The *idea* of elevated road is developed into the idea of difficulty of locating station, length of time occupied on the journey, distance of station at the other end from place to be reached. In the second case, the implication of a flagpole is seen to be a vertical position; of a wireless apparatus, location on a high part of the ship and, moreover, absence from every casual tugboat; while the idea of index to direction in which the boat moves, when developed, is found to cover all the details of the case.

Reasoning has the same effect upon a suggested solution as more intimate and extensive observation has upon the original problem. Acceptance of the suggestion in its first form is prevented by looking into it more thoroughly. Conjectures that seem plausible at first sight are often found unfit or even absurd when their full consequences are traced out. Even when reasoning out the bearings of a supposition does not lead to rejection, it develops the idea into a form in which it is more apposite to the problem. Only when, for example, the conjecture that a pole was an index pole had been thought out into its bearings could its particular applicability to the case in hand be judged. Suggestions at first seemingly remote and wild are frequently so transformed by being elaborated into what follows from them as to become apt and fruitful. The development of an idea through reasoning helps at least to supply the intervening or intermediate terms that link together into a consistent whole apparently discrepant extremes.

(5) The concluding and conclusive step is some kind of *experimental corroboration*, or verification, of the conjectural idea. Reasoning shows that *if* the idea be adopted, certain consequences follow. So far the conclusion is hypothetical or conditional. If we look and find present all the conditions demanded by the theory, and if we find the characteristic traits

called for by rival alternatives to be lacking, the tendency to believe, to accept, is almost irresistible. Sometimes direct observation furnishes corroboration, as in the case of the pole on the boat. In other cases, as in that of the bubbles, experiment is required; that is, *conditions are deliberately arranged in accord with the requirements of an idea or hypothesis to see if the results theoretically indicated by the idea actually occur.* If it is found that the experimental results agree with the theoretical, or rationally deduced, results, and if there is reason to believe that *only* the conditions in question would yield such results, the confirmation is so strong as to induce a conclusion—at least until contrary facts shall indicate the advisability of its revision.

Observation exists at the beginning and again at the end of the process: at the beginning, to determine more definitely and precisely the nature of the difficulty to be dealt with; at the end, to test the value of some hypothetically entertained conclusion. Between those two termini of observation, we find the more distinctively *mental* aspects of the entire thought cycle: (i) inference, the suggestion of an explanation or solution; and (ii) reasoning, the development of the bearings and implications of the suggestion. Reasoning requires some experimental observation to confirm it, while experiment can be economically and fruitfully conducted only on the basis of an idea that has been tentatively developed by reasoning.

The disciplined, or logically trained, mind—the aim of the educative process—is the mind able to judge how far each of these steps needs to be carried in any particular situation. No cast-iron rules can be laid down. Each case has to be dealt with as it arises, on the basis of its importance and of the context in which it occurs. To take too much pains in one case is as foolish—as illogical—as to take too little in another. At one extreme, almost any conclusion that insures prompt and unified action may be better than any long-delayed conclusion; while at the other, decision may have to be postponed for a long period—perhaps for a lifetime. The trained mind is the one that best grasps the degree of observation, forming of ideas, reasoning, and experimental testing required in any special case, and that profits the most, in future thinking, by mistakes made in the past. What is important is that the mind should be sensitive to problems and skilled in methods of attack and solution.

1) Analyze some problem-solving activity of your own in the light of Dewey's analysis.
2) In what way does Dewey's analysis of thought suggest a method for handling Bacon's "idols"?
3) Would Plato, do you think, be satisfied with Dewey's analysis?

THE MECHANISM OF LANGUAGE

THE mind gets so used to certain symbols, such as Hercules standing for strength, that it comes as something of a shock to find him described as an old, wizened man. But Lucian, a Greek rhetorician of the second century, wrote that the Gauls pictured him as an old man who

> draws men along with their ears tied to his tongue . . . with thin chains composed of gold and amber . . . From this flimsy bondage they make no attempt to escape, though escape must be easy. There is not the slightest show of resistance: instead of planting their heels in the ground and dragging back, they follow with joyful alacrity, singing their captor's praises the while; and from the eagerness with which they hurry after him to prevent the chains from tightening, one would say that release is the last thing that they desire.

Lucian explains why the Gauls had such an unusual picture of Hercules: they recognized that physical strength is nothing compared to the power of language. If Hercules were truly to represent strength, his strength had to rest in his tongue. The chains are the chains of words which hold captive the minds of men.

Someone who is color-blind is involved in many difficulties, and someone blind to errors in his use of language may be involved in unforeseen difficulties which only knowledge of language processes will help him avoid. A sense of humor prevented any misunderstanding of the request made to the insurance company: "Please send me my wife's form to fill out." When, as here, the difference between sense and non-sense is obvious, no real difficulty exists, but it does exist when the absurdity is not obvious. It is said that the Light Brigade charged to its doom at the Battle of Balaclava because "some-one had blundered." The blunder was due to a misinterpreta-tion of the direction, "There, my Lord, is your enemy." The ambiguity in the word *there* resulted in the commander of the Light Brigade attacking the wrong Russian position. The men of the Light Brigade died because of a word, and history is full of examples of men who have died in the name of words whose meaning is vague or nonexistent. Language, therefore, seems to have strange qualities of its own. These qualities we seek to discover and examine.

LANGUAGE IS A MEANS OF COMMUNICATION

The first and most obvious characteristic about language is that it is a *means* of communicating ideas. Yet people con-stantly ignore the obvious fact that language is, so to speak, the milk bottle, not the milk inside the bottle. Although language is obviously not the same thing as what it communi-cates, words are frequently regarded as if they themselves—the mere sounds—were things with special unique powers. Yet a moment's reflection should make it obvious that words are no more than mere sounds which are chosen by human beings to symbolize meanings that are external to them. Words can refer to things, but they are not themselves things.

Ignorance of the symbolic nature of words has led to curious superstitions. People have often believed that the word *is* the thing, and that to possess power over the word is to have magical control over the thing. In fairy tales heroes are always looking for strange combinations of words that will cause sudden events. And witches are able to call up all kinds of diabolical creatures merely by saying the proper words. Savage communities attach great importance to words. Frequently they give a child a "real" name known only to the family, and also a "social" name by which he is known to the community. His "real" name is disguised so as to prevent an enemy from controlling the child by means of the name. The person and the name are regarded as one and the same. Not only savages, but also civilized men have believed in the reality of language. Not too long ago the Cambridge city fathers attempted to keep their city safe from communism by banning the use of the word *communism* within the city limits.

To understand more exactly what is meant by saying that language is primarily a means of communication, consider a simple language situation. A person is sitting at the dinner table. At the far end is a platter of potatoes that he wants. He could, of course, get up, walk around the table, and bring the platter back to his place. In this simple situation he would have no need for language. But imagine the resultant chaos if he could obtain what he wanted only by direct action. He would be required to do everything for himself. Buildings, automobiles, and all the rest could never be constructed because to make them requires shared activities made possible only by language. Language, therefore, is the primary means by which human beings get things done. It is probably the most essential activity involved in being a human, for civilization could not long exist without language.

Unfortunately language is not always used correctly. It is misused when people forget to ask what language is communicating and assume that because language sounds "right" it must mean something. Read the following description of nature by the great American writer Samuel Clemens:

It was a crisp and spicy morning in early October. The lilacs and laburnams, lit with the glory fires of autumn, hung burning and flashing in the upper air, a fairy bridge provided by kind Nature for the wingless wild things that have their home in the tree tops and would visit together; the larch and the pomegranate flung their purple and yellow flames in brilliant broad splashes along the slanting sweep of the woodland; the sensuous fragrance of innumerable deciduous flowers rose upon the swooning atmosphere; far in the empty sky a solitary oesophagus slept upon motionless wing; everywhere brooded stillness, serenity, and the peace of God.

Unless you are unusually analytical, even though you were forewarned, you did not perceive, as you read, that the whole passage is a deliberately contrived tissue of nonsense. The usual response is conditioned by ingrained habits. You knew the passage was written by a famous author. More important, the passage probably "sounded good" to you. Although you may not have grasped the meaning of a few words, you felt, vaguely, that the sounds "made sense."

What has happened in your reading—and especially in your reciting—of Clemens's description is what happens only too frequently in all reading and listening. Rhythmic patterns have an effect. A resonant voice holds attention. Thus radio commentators are famed, and announcers are paid large salaries because their voices sound "sincere," "friendly," or "exciting," no matter what they are saying.

LANGUAGE IS A CREATION OF HUMAN SOCIETY

Because language is a means of communication, evoking responses in a listener, it cannot exist in isolation. Sounds become a language because there are individuals who regard these sounds as more than mere noises. The sounds become signs of actions to be performed or considered. But imagine if instead of saying "pass the potatoes" someone said, *"Les pommes de terre, s'il vous plaît."* Assume that the listener does not understand French; he would be hearing noises which would not constitute a language for him. These sounds might appear to belong to a language because he once heard some

French spoken, or because the sounds resemble ones he is himself accustomed to use. But a language actually exists only
when two or more human beings are able to give similar
interpretations to the sounds. "Please pass the potatoes" is a
series of sounds that belong to a language, English, because
they have received similar interpretations by many human
beings.

To say that a language exists when many give similar interpretations to certain sounds does not mean that there is one
and only one way to refer to something. When a social group
agrees in calling an object *tree*, this sound is "correct" for that
group. But if another group agrees in calling this object *baum*,
the sound *baum* would be just as correct for that group as
the sound *tree* is for the other. There is no absolutely correct
way of speaking, as Jim believed when he objected to Huck
Finn's statement that the Frenchman says, "Polly-voo-franzy?"
instead of "Do you speak French?" Jim replied:

"Well, den, why couldn't he say it?"

"Why, he *is* a-saying it. That's a Frenchman's way of
saying it."

"Well, it's a blame ridicklous way, en I doan' want to
hear no mo' 'bout it. Day ain' no sense in it."

"Loky here, Jim; does a cat talk like we do?"

"No, a cat don't."

"Well, does a cow?"

"No, a cow don't, nuther."

"Does a cat talk like a cow, or a cow talk like a cat?"

"No, they don't."

"It's natural and right for 'em to talk different from
each other, ain't it?"

"Course."

"And ain't it natural and right for a cat and a cow to
talk different from *us?*"

"Why, mos' sholy it is."

"Well, then, why ain't it natural and right for a Frenchman to talk different from us? You answer me that."

"Is a cat a man, Huck?"

"No."

"Well, den dey ain't no sense in a cat talkin' like a man. Is a cow a man? —er is a cow a cat?"

"No, she ain't either of them."

"Well, den, she ain't got no business to talk like either one er the yuther of 'em. Is a Frenchman a man?"

"Yes."

"Well, den! Dad blame it, why doan' he talk like a man? You answer me dat!"

On the other hand, because no one set of sounds is more correct than another, it does not follow that anyone can arbitrarily decide to use his own language or his own meanings. Admittedly no policeman forces compliance with a specific way of speaking, but if anyone insisted on using his own language, he would communicate only with himself. What would result if language were left entirely to individual initiative is amusingly illustrated in Alice's conversation with Humpty Dumpty:

"I don't know what you mean by 'glory,'" Alice said.

Humpty Dumpty smiled contemptuously. "Of course you don't—till I tell you. I meant 'there's a nice knock-down argument for you!'"

"But 'glory' doesn't mean 'a nice knock-down argument,'" Alice objected.

"When I use a word," Humpty Dumpty said, in rather a scornful tone, "it means just what I choose it to mean— neither more nor less."

"The question is," said Alice, "whether you *can* make words mean so many different things."

"The question is," said Humpty Dumpty, "which is to be master—that's all."

Alice was too much puzzled to say anything; so after a minute Humpty Dumpty began again. "They've a temper, some of them—particularly verbs: they're the proudest— adjectives you can do anything with, but not verbs—however, I can manage the whole lot of them! Impenetrability: That's what I say!"

"Would you tell me please," said Alice, "what that means?"

"Now you talk like a reasonable child," said Humpty Dumpty, looking very much pleased. "I meant by 'impenetrability' that we've had enough of that subject, and it would be just as well if you'd mention what you mean to do next, as I suppose you don't mean to stop here all the rest of your life."

"That's a great deal to make one word mean," Alice said in a thoughtful tone.

"When I make a word do a lot of work like that," said Humpty Dumpty, "I always pay it extra."

"OH!" said Alice. She was much too puzzled to make any other remark.

"Ah, you should see 'em come round me of a Saturday night," Humpty Dumpty went on, wagging his head gravely from side to side, "for to get their wages, you know."

Humpty Dumpty has fallen into the fallacy of believing that he, as an individual, can make up his own language. But he is still constrained to use English words such as *glory* and *impenetrability*. More than this, Humpty Dumpty shows that he must accept conventional meanings if he really wishes to communicate to anyone. Thus language is man-made, but is not made by one man.

To many, perhaps most, people language seems natural, not man-made and conventional. Most of us have the attitude that language is "natural" because we cannot remember a time when we were without speech. But actually language is a habit that is learned through the constant repetition of particular sound patterns. Anyone learning a foreign language will recall repeating over and over the basic vocabulary and grammatical patterns. Finally constant repetition fixed these patterns firmly enough in mind so that their use became automatic. No longer did the learner have to say to himself, "Now what is the French word for 'you'?" Instead, the French *vous* or *tu* came without effort. In acquiring our own language we went through a similar learning process between the ages of nine to thirty months. We do not recall this occurrence because our memories do not go back far enough. But the harassed mother of a two-year-old will testify that the young child spends a great deal of time learning his language.

Nor is the fact that man is born with "vocal organs" evidence that he is endowed with an innate urge to speak. Enormously serviceable as are the vocal organs in producing the subtlest modifications in sound, highly adaptable as they are, *not one of them is designed simply to be a vocal organ.* Here is a primary and startling fact about language. Our lungs were designed to transmit oxygen to the blood stream, and the nose and mouth to permit the air to reach the lungs. The tongue, the teeth, the palate, the mouth were designed either for fighting or for eating. The complicated mechanism of the larynx (see chart) and the so-called vocal cords have their primary purpose, not in the producing of sound, but rather in controlling the air pressure in the lungs. As R.M.S. Heffner (*General Phonetics,* p. 23) points out:

> This mechanism is essential to normal elimination from the alimentary canal and it plays an important part in normal childbirth . . . If this mechanism did not exist, the nature and extent of our arm efforts would be drastically restricted. A great many of the muscular actions of our arms depend upon the creation of a partial vacuum beneath the vocal bands. Without these two valvular controls of the opening of the larynx [vocal cords] the human animal would have very little power above the hips. He could not lift himself, or any object of size, with his arms.

Since the vocal organs were not by nature designed for speech, man must in some remarkable way have invented language.

LANGUAGE IS BUILT UP FROM SOUND UNITS CALLED "PHONEMES"

The sound organs which man employs in such a remarkable way in order to create sound are shown in the following schematic cross-section of the human head:

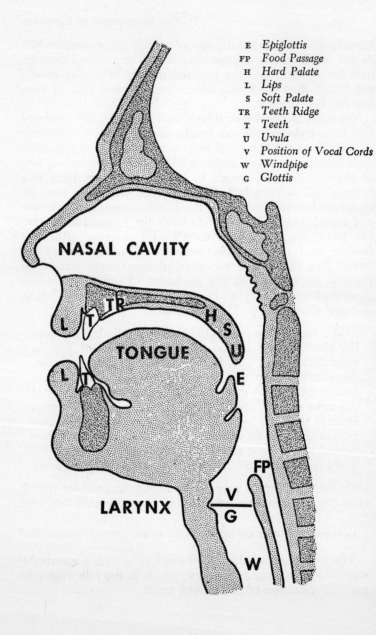

E   *Epiglottis*
FP *Food Passage*
H   *Hard Palate*
L   *Lips*
S   *Soft Palate*
TR *Teeth Ridge*
T   *Teeth*
U   *Uvula*
V   *Position of Vocal Cords*
W   *Windpipe*
G   *Glottis*

The sounds of speech are produced by these vocal organs. Breath is expelled from the lungs and passes through the *larynx*. In the larynx are two cords, called the *vocal cords*. When these are relaxed, the breath passes through the larynx unmodified, but when the cords are tightened, a vibration is caused which we call *voice*. When the vocal cords are relaxed, the resultant sound is said to be *unvoiced*; when tightened, the sound is said to be *voiced*. As the stream of breath, *voiced* or *unvoiced*, comes to the back of the mouth, it may be directed in one of two paths, through the nose or through the mouth. The English sounds *m, n, -ing* are made by directing the voiced breath stream through the *nose*. The other English sounds are made by the breath stream passing through the mouth. The breath stream, voiced or unvoiced, is further modified by the position of the *tongue*, of the *teeth*, or of the *lips*. The sound in English *b* (as in *bin*) is made by the voiced breath stream being stopped momentarily by the lips. The sound *m* is made with the lips in position for *b*, but with the voiced breath directed through the nose. People with colds have difficulty directing breath through the nose so that their *m*'s sound something like *b*. English *p* (as in *pin*) is identical with *b* except that the breath stream is unvoiced; that is to say, the vocal cords are relaxed.

The basic speech sounds created by human beings are not always easy to discern. The written alphabet began as an attempt to record the speech sounds of a given language. But the correlation between the alphabet and the sounds of Modern English no longer holds. Three of the letters, *c, k,* and *q* represent the same sound. The letter *x* represents no distinct sound; rather it represents the sound of *k* (or *g*) combined with *s* as in *Xray* and *extra*. Some letters represent more than one sound, as does the *a* in the following: *fat, father, ate, deliberate,* and *China*. Consequently, the linguist who wishes to get at the actual speech sounds of English (or any other language) cannot rely on the alphabet.

Instead, the linguist listens to people speaking. He notes the sounds which the speakers of the language actually use. By listening and analyzing what he hears he begins to isolate words, that is, basic combinations of sound units, for example, *tin*. He notes that this word consists of three distinct sounds, *t-i-n*. He observes that if a sound such as *d* is substituted for *t*, a new word is made: *t* and *d* are, therefore, distinctive units of interchangeable sound. If *a* or *e* is substituted for the *i* in *tin*, a new word is made: *a* and *e* are distinctive sound units. By listening carefully the linguist finally records all the distinctive units of sound in the language under study. These distinctive units of sound the linguist calls *phonemes*. The term *phoneme* is of primary importance to designate the irreducible, distinctive, interchangeable unit of sound.

Discovering the phonemes of a language is not, however, as easy as it seems. Sounds vary from person to person and even from word to word. In the final test two sounds must be considered as belonging to the same phoneme if one sound can be substituted for the other without any real change of meaning in any words in which the sound occurs. If the *g* of *got* is replaced by the *g* in *get*, the word still retains its original meaning. On the other hand, if the sound *d* replaces the sound *t* in *tin* we have a new word with a new meaning. In English, for example, there are two distinct *g* and two distinct *c* [k] sounds. The difference may be heard by pronouncing *get—got, catch—caught*. In *get* the *g* is pronounced toward the front of the mouth, the *g* in *got* toward the back of the mouth. The same holds true for the *c* [k] in *catch* and *caught*. In *catch* the *c* [k] is said frontally; in *caught* it is said with the tongue moving backward. But they are still considered to be instances of the same sound, viz., the phoneme [k]. The phoneme, therefore, is more exactly described as a distinctive area of sound, sometimes comprising two or more fairly different sounds, as with *g* in *got* and *g* in *get*, which can be substituted in various words without any change of meaning in those words.

Even though there is no longer a strict correlation between phonemes and the letters of the alphabet, the phonemes are, to a large extent, the basis of the written language of today. Probably, however, writing originated, not as a transcription of sound, but rather as a transcription of events, especially those events which the group as a whole wished to glorify. For this reason the ancient Egyptians, the ancient Chinese, and the American Indians used a pictorial kind of writing. But pictorial writing is very hard to manage, as may be illustrated by Chinese ideographic writing which evolved from a pictorial system. To learn Chinese writing the beginner must learn some 214 distinct signs.

On the other hand, most writing today is based on a different principle. Each written sign approximately represents (or did originally) a distinct sound rather than a picture. The word *pig* is composed of three letters each of which represents a sound; in combination these letters represent the sound of the word *pig*. Modern writing is thus freed from the limitations of pictorial representations; it has something of the flexibility of sound itself, and this flexibility has given writing a much greater value than is possible in a pictorial system. As a result of a complex of events, including the invention of the printing press, universal education, and the rise of democracies, the use of writing has become commonplace. The effect of this has been gradually to divorce writing from speech, so that people are sometimes surprised to learn that writing is based upon speech. It is, however, a serious mistake not to recognize the basic importance of spoken language, since except for perhaps highly technical matters, understanding the written language is dependent on understanding the spoken language.

THE PHONEMES OF HUMAN LANGUAGE ARE NOT COMPARABLE TO THE SOUNDS MADE BY ANIMALS

If the noises of an animal and the speech of man were compared, a crucial difference would be found. Whereas a man can choose sounds to stand for objects, the animal never chooses its sounds. For example, note the difference between the word *cat* and a cat's *meow*. The human word is made up of a series of phonemes, units of interchangeable sound; the sounds the animal makes are never interchangeable. The phonemes of *cat*, *c-a-t*, may be and are changed around, as in *act*, *a-c-t*, a combination of the same phonemes found in *cat*, but in the new combination meaning something different. The animal does not employ interchangeable units of sound: there are no phonemes in animal speech. The cat says *meow*, but not *owme*. The basic sounds of animals are fixed in position, whereas those of human beings are varied in an indefinite number of combinations. Even though animals may seem to have a number of distinct basic sound units, such sounds do not have the crucial characteristic of interchangeability.

A sharp limit is set to animal speech, but no limits are set to the number of different messages that language can communicate. Yet the primary means language employs, phonemes, are very few. English, for example, has less than forty-five phonemes. Thus, on the one hand, is the vast, limitless number of experiences to which language may refer; on the other hand is a handful of distinctive sounds which, in combination, comprise the human language. The significant facts about the phoneme are that it is distinct from all other phonemes and that it has no fixed meaning. The word peg has "meaning," but the individual sounds *p-e-g* do not. Change the last phoneme in *peg* to *t* and a new word is formed, *pet*, even though *t* has no meaning in itself. Thus the units of sound in language have no prescribed meaning and can be combined in numerous different ways. These characteristics distinguish human speech from animal speech and account for the great versatility of human speech. Indeed words are created so constantly and so rapidly that dictionaries soon would be out-of-date if "new word" sections were not added to them every few years.

The significance of having a language whose basic sounds are meaningless becomes apparent when we consider what would occur if such basic units did have individual meanings. Either we would face the impossible task of finding a different sound for every object to which we wished to refer, or we would have to form all new words by combining sounds that have already been given meanings of their own. Imagine the confusion! It would be as if there were a language of a limitless number of sounds, or a language of forty to fifty basic words from which all other words would have to be formed. In the latter event, each new word would have two meanings: (1) that of its component parts, and (2) that of the word as a whole. The ambiguity inherent in language would become unmanageable. On the other hand, with forty or fifty basic *meaningless* sounds, phonemes, a tremendous number of new words can be formed without the confusion of having to include sounds that already have a meaning.

WORDS ARE SELECTED SETS OF PHONEMES WHICH HAVE BEEN GIVEN MEANING

Words are formed by combining phonemes into different arrangements. However, this does not imply that any combination of phonemes will be a word. First of all, some combinations are not allowable. Thus, we "accept" a word that ends in *ng*, for example, *sing, swing*; we do not accept as English a word that begins with this sound. The single-syllable word may begin with any other consonant, which in turn may be followed immediately by any vowel: *pat, pet, pit, pot, put*. But very strict and particularized limits are set for consonant sequences. The initial *p* may be followed only by *l* and *r*, as in *pray, plum*, and by a glide sound *y* as in *pew*. A word beginning *pd, pk*, would not be accepted as English. Again no consonant sequence with initial *s* is permitted except *sp, st, sk, sw, sl*, as in *spin, sting, swing, sling*. Elaborately different conventions apply to the combinations of all the phonemes of English. In fact, the linguist Benjamin Lee Whorf has pointed out that it is possible to devise a formula which will show all the possible ways of combining phonemes that are permitted in Modern English. (See Exercise 3 in this chapter.)

Second, even if a combination of phonemes is allowable, it may not be a word. As Alice discovered when she read the poem *Jabberwocky*, combinations of sounds may seem familiar and meaningful, but they do not always comprise a genuine word:

> 'Twas brillig and the slithy toves
> Did gyre and gimble in the wabe:

> All mimsy were the borogoves,
>> And the mome raths outgrabe. . . .

When Alice finished the poem of which this is the first stanza, she felt puzzled; at the same time she was sure that it meant something:

> It seems very pretty . . . but it is hard to understand . . . Somehow it seems to fill my head with ideas—only I don't exactly know what they are!

Alice couldn't quite understand the meanings of most of the "words" in the poem. Yet paradoxically all the sounds were organized in arrangements which are allowable in the English language. *Mimsy, toves, mome,* etc. satisfy the formal require-ments of English words. But although they sound like English words, we do not accept them as such because they lack a prime requisite—recognizable meaning. Thus not all combina-tions of sounds are words. A specific combination of sounds becomes a word when it has been given a meaning.

The primary operation of language involves learning to use a handful of distinctive sounds in recognizable patterns to which meaning is attached. The process of learning to speak starts when the child begins to imitate. Language, in conse-quence, becomes a habit which ordinarily requires no conscious effort. For this reason language can become treacherous. Taking advantage of the power of sound and of undiscriminating lan-guage habits, the demagogue sways people to his will, binds them with the golden chain of Hercules. The very economy of language and the ease with which a child acquires it give language both its value and its danger.

EXERCISES

1. (*a*) *Have someone read the following passage aloud as if he were engaged in normal rapid conversation:*
It is raining outside, but I've got to go home anyway because if I don't I'll catch it for being late for supper. I'll call you

tomorrow afternoon if I don't see you in the morning. Maybe we can go to the movies if we don't have too much work to do: anyway we can make some fudge.

(b) *Try to transcribe* what you actually hear, *using the phonetic symbols described in your dictionary.*

(c) *List the* phonemes *that you actually hear.*

(d) *Do you find any significant differences between what is written and what you hear?*

(e) *Are the "word patterns" of the written passage the same as those you hear? Comment.*

(f) *For further study transcribe conversations, using a tape recorder.*

------

2. *What principles of language are illustrated in the following? Comment on each.*

(a) *"How to Bark Abroad," by Leslie Lieber and Charles D. Rice from* This Week, *1953.*

Leafing through a book in the Italian language the other day, we were suddenly brought up short by the following passage: "The little dog ran through the streets of Naples barking *boo-boo, boo-boo, boo-boo* at all the passersby."

We expected the next sentence to announce that this dog who spouted *boo-boo* had been whisked away to the nearest canine psycho ward for observation. But when the author failed to comment on this pooch's peculiar behavior, a disconcerting thought dawned on us.

Could it be that all the world doesn't see eye-to-eye on the fact that dogs say either *bow-wow* or *woof-woof*? Deciding that this question merited a survey, we immediately phoned the Italian Embassy in Washington. A chargé d'affaires refused point-blank to bark over the telephone. Finally, however, an underling agreed to bark. It came through sharp and unmistakable: *boo-boo, boo-boo* (spelled in Italian *bu-bu*).

The news that 45,000,000 Italians are convinced their dogs bark like Bing Crosby was provocative enough to warrant a full-scale investigation of the whole international barnyard.

We must admit that our hopes for world unity have not been greatly heartened by our findings. Take the cow, for instance. *Moo* is American. The French have the piquant notion that Bossy gives out with a nasal *meuh* (pronounced as "mur" in demur). In India, a country where cows are sacred, they never say *moo*. Ganges cows say *moe* (rhymes with schmoe).

Frankly we don't know what to make of the rooster situation. But we'll tell you one thing: the rest of the world is sharply opposed to us in the *cock-a-doodle-do* department. Germany, Spain and Italy are all agreed that what this bird is trying to say is *kikiriki* (kee-kee-ree-kee), *quiquiriqui* and *chicchiricchi*, respectively. In Spanish-speaking countries, young roosters say *quiquiriqui*, but the old ones go *quiquiriqoooo*. France deviates slightly in favor of *cocorico*; Japan votes for *kokekkoko*—all far cries from *cock-a-doodle-do*.

Most of the Western world goes along with the U. S. conviction that ducks quack. But you can't argue a Chinese out of the certainty that Cantonese ducks say *ap-ap*. Ducks in Japan go around spouting *ga-ga*; Arabic ones—*bat-bat*; Rumanian—*mac-mac*. If you should ever go duck hunting in Germany and hear a *quack-quack*, don't be too quick to shoot. In Germany, ducks go *quack-quack* all right—but so do frogs.

In their native habitat, Spanish cockers say *how-how* (jau-jau written in Castilian). French poodles in Alsace sit on the banks of the Rhine barking *oua-oua* (wa-wa), while lonely Dachshunds staring back at them from the German side fill the air with *vau-vau, vau-vau, vau-vau* (vow-vow). The Turks are under the impression that their hounds say *hov-hov, hov-hov*. Nor is there any arguing with the Russians. Wolf-hounds invented barking. And believe it or not, dogs in Moscow gather around the Kremlin at night and bay *vas-vas, vas-vas* at the moon. It is in China, however, that the canine kingdom goes completely berserk. Their dogs say *wang-wang, wang-wang*.

We asked our Russian informant whether Soviet children ever sing a song entitled, "Old MacDonald Had a Collectivized Farm, Ee-i, Ee-i, O." This ditty, it appears, does not exist behind the Iron Curtain. And it's just as well, we say, for it would sound like this: "With a *vas-vas* here a *h'roo-h'roo* there, here a *vas*, there a *vas*, everywhere a *vas-vas*."

We wouldn't like to conclude without mentioning one encouraging sign on the horizon: the Nutka Indians of Vancouver Island claim that whales say *hux* under normal conditions and *peu-wu* when excited. Surprisingly enough, the Russian Eskimos living on the Siberian side of the Bering Strait are in perfect accord with the capitalistic Nutka tribe on this point.

From the mouth of a whale, then, comes our brightest promise of world accord. His *hux* is the only fact on earth regarding animal sounds which observers accept without a quibble. If some day we could all attune our ears to accept *hux* as belonging to the whale—and not to the otter, the sloth or the Afghanistan loom—it might be the rallying point for a glorious era of peace on earth and good will between men and all the animals in the zoo.

(*b*) *Sam Clemens's "Jumping Frog" in French.*
Sam Clemens once read a French article on American humor in which a translation of his story "The Jumping Frog" appeared, as Clemens says, "in order to prove to his nation that there is nothing so extravagantly funny about it." Clemens felt moved to reply: in his article he first gives his original story, then the French version, and finally a beautifully absurd literal translation of the French. He concludes:

Such is the Jumping Frog, to the distorted French eye. I claim that I never put together such an odious mixture of bad grammar and delirium tremens in my life. And what has a poor foreigner like me done, to be abused and misrepresented like this? When I say, "Well, I don't see no p'ints about that frog that's any better'n any other frog," is it kind, is it just, for this Frenchman to try to make it appear that I said, "Eh bien! I no saw not that that frog had nothing of better than each frog?" I have no heart to write more. I never felt so about anything before.

(*c*) *Doctor Faustus summons the Devil (from Marlowe's* Doctor Faustus):

Faustus, begin thine incantations,
And try if devils will obey thy hest,
Seeing thou hast prayed and sacrificed to them.
Within this circle is Jehovah's name,
Forward and backward anagrammatized,
The breviated names of holy saints,
Figures of every adjunct to the heavens,
And characters of signs and erring stars,
By which the spirits are enforced to rise.

(d) Animal Communication
Emile Beneviste in "Animal Communication" (Diogenes
I, 1–7) *tells of experiments which show that bees are apparently able to communicate with one another by means of gestures:*

Karl von Frisch . . . has observed the conduct of the bee returning after the discovery of honey. It is immediately surrounded by the others. The excitement of the hive is great. They stretch out their antennae towards it to collect the pollen with which it is laden or they drink the nectar which it disgorges. Then, followed by the others, the scouting bee proceeds to perform dances. This is the critical moment and constitutes the act of communication.

But Beneviste claims that the bees cannot be said to have language, because their means of communication consists in "a dance, without the intervention of any vocal organ, whereas there can be no real language without the exercise of voice."

(e) Selling Handkerchiefs

Experiments were made in a department store to determine the effectiveness of various displays. In one experiment two identical batches of handkerchiefs were put on opposite counters. One batch was advertised:

Imported Linen Handkerchiefs
Special Close-Out: 25 cents each

The other: Useful Pocket-Rags
Fair Price: $1.00 for six

None of the latter batch was sold: a brisk sale was made of the former batch.

---

3. *The following excerpt from an article by B. L. Whorf sets up a formula for the pattern of the monosyllabic word. Read the excerpt carefully. Make sure you understand the formula by testing your ability to use it, giving, for example, the formula for several of the "nonsense" words in the Jabberwocky poem, toves, etc. Show that these actually do have the pattern of English words. Consider the implications of Whorf's remarks about the structure of language.*

A STRUCTURAL FORMULA FROM "LINGUISTICS AS AN
EXACT SCIENCE" BY BENJAMIN LEE WHORF

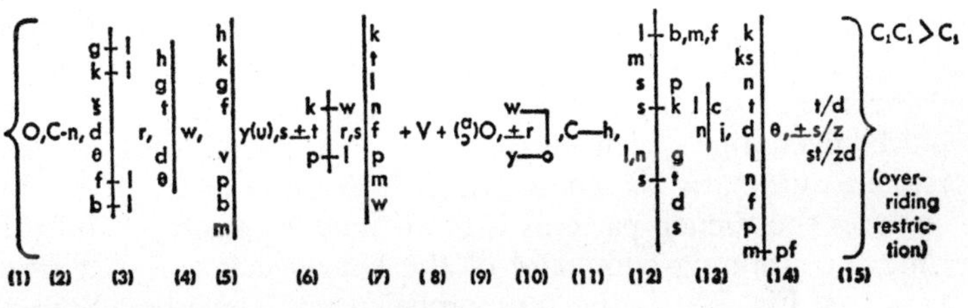

FIGURE 1 [1]

The structural formula for words of one syllable in the English language (Fig. 1) looks rather complicated; yet for a linguistic pattern it is rather simple. In the English-speaking world, every child between the ages of two and five is engaged in learning the pattern expressed by this formula, among many other formulas. By the time the child is six, the formula has become ingrained and automatic; even the little nonsense words the child makes up conform to it, exploring its possibilities but venturing not a jot beyond them. At an early age the formula becomes for the child what it is for the adult; no

[1] Reprinted by permission from *Language, Thought, and Reality*, Selected Writings of Benjamin Lee Whorf. New York, 1956. The Technology Press of M.I.T. and John Wiley & Sons, Inc.

sequence of sounds that deviates from it can even be articulated without the greatest difficulty. New words like "blurb," nonsense words like Lewis Carroll's "mome raths," combinations intended to suggest languages of savages or animal cries, like "glub" and "squonk"—all come out of the mold of this formula. When the youth begins to learn a foreign language, he unconsciously tries to construct the syllables according to his formula. Of course it won't work; the foreign words are built to a formula of their own. Usually the student has a terrible time. Not even knowing that a formula is back of all the trouble, he thinks his difficulty is his own fault. The frustrations and inhibitions thus set up at the start constantly block his attempts to use foreign tongues. Or else he even *hears* by the formula, so that the English combinations that he makes sound to him like real French, for instance. Then he suffers less inhibition and may become what is called a "fluent" speaker of French—bad French!

If, however, he is so fortunate as to have his elementary French taught by a theoretic linguist, he first has the patterns of the English formula explained in such a way that they become semiconscious, with the result that they lose the binding power over him which custom has given them, though they remain automatic as far as English is concerned. Then he acquires the French patterns without inner opposition, and the time for attaining command of the language is cut to a fraction (see Fig. 2). To be sure, probably no elementary French is ever taught in this way—at least not in public institutions. Years of time and millions of dollars' worth of wasted educational effort could be saved by the adoption of such methods, but men with the grounding in theoretic linguistics are as yet far too few and are chiefly in the higher institutions.

Let us examine the formula for the English monosyllabic word. It looks mathematical, but it isn't. It is an expression of pattern symbolics, an analytical method that grows out of linguistics and bears to linguistics a relation not unlike that of higher mathematics to physics. With such pattern formulas various operations can be performed, just as mathematical expressions can be added, multiplied, and otherwise operated

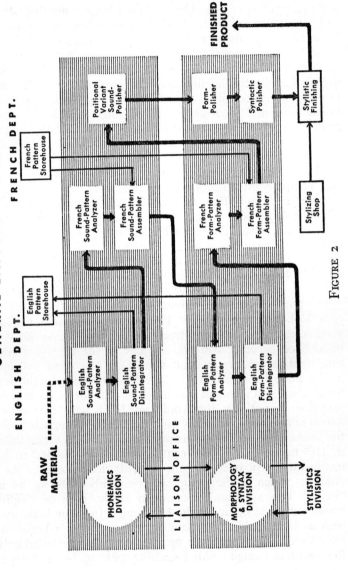

FIGURE 2

with; only the operations here are not addition, multiplication, and so on, but are meanings that apply to linguistic contexts. From these operations conclusions can be drawn and experimental attacks directed intelligently at the really crucial points in the welter of data presented by the language under investigation. Usually the linguist does not need to manipulate the formulas on paper but simply performs the symbolic operations in his mind and then says: "The paradigm of Class A verbs can't have been reported right by the previous investigator"; or "Well, well, this language must have alternating stresses, though I couldn't hear them at first"; or "Funny, but d and l must be variants of the same sound in this language," and so on. Then he investigates by experimenting on a native informant and finds that the conclusion is justified. Pattern-symbolic expressions are exact, as mathematics is, but are not quantitative. They do not refer ultimately to number and dimension, as mathematics does, but to pattern and structure. Nor are they to be confused with theory of groups or with symbolic logic, though they may be in some ways akin.

Returning to the formula, the simplest part of it is the eighth term (the terms are numbered underneath), consisting of a V between plus signs. This means that every English word contains a vowel (not true of all languages). As the V is unqualified by other symbols, any one of the English vowels can occur in the monosyllabic word (not true of all syllables of the polysyllabic English word). Next we turn to the first term, which is a zero and which means that the vowel may be preceded by nothing; the word may begin with a vowel—a structure impossible in many languages. The commas between the terms mean "or." The second term is C minus a long-tailed n. This means that a word can begin with any single English consonant except one—the one linguists designate by a long-tailed n, which is the sound we commonly write ng, as in "hang." This ng sound is common at the ends of English words but never occurs at the beginnings. In many languages, such as Hopi, Eskimo, or Samoan, it is a common beginning for a word. Our patterns set up a terrific resistance to articulation of these foreign words beginning with ng, but as soon as the mechanism of producing *ng* has been explained and we learn that our inability has been due to a habitual pattern, we can place the *ng* wherever we will and can pronounce these words with the greatest of ease. The letters in the formula thus are not always equivalent to the letters by which we express our words in ordinary spelling but are unequivocal symbols such as a linguist would assign to the sounds in a regular and scientific system of spelling.

According to the third term, which consists of two columns, the word can begin with any consonant of the first column followed by *r*, or with *g*, *k*, *f*, or *b* followed by *l*. The *s* with a wedge over it means *sh*. Thus we have "shred," but not "shled." The formula represents the fact that "shled" is un-English, that it will suggest a Chinese's pronunciation of "shred" or a German's of "sled" (*sl* is permitted by term 7). The Greek theta means *th*; so we have "thread" but not "thled," which latter suggests either a Chinese saying "thread" or a child lisping "sled." But why aren't *tr*, *pr*, and *pl* in this third term? Because they can be preceded by *s* and so belong in term 6. The fourth term similarly means that the word can begin with a consonant of the first column followed by *w*. *Hw* does not occur in all dialects of English; in ordinary spelling it is written backward, *wh*. If the dialect does not have *hw*, it pronounces the spelled *wh* simply as *w*. *Thw* occurs in a few words, like "thwack" and "thwart," and *gw*, oddly enough, only in proper names, like Gwen or Gwynn. *Kw*, ordinarily spelled *qu*, can have *s* before it and therefore belongs in term 6.

The fifth term indicates that the word may begin with one of the first-column consonants followed by *y*, but only when the vowel of the word is *u*; thus we have words like "hue" (*hyuw*), "cue," "few," "muse." Some dialects have also *tyu*, *dyu*, and *nyu* (e.g., in "tune," "due," and "new"), but I have set up the formula for the typical dialects of the northern United States which have simple *tu*, *du*, *nu* in these words. The sixth term indicates pairs that can commence a word either alone or preceded by *s*, that is, *k*, *t*, or *p* followed by *r*, also *kw* and *pl* (think of "train," "strain"; "crew," "screw"; "quash," "squash"; "play," "splay"). The seventh term, which means

the word can begin with *s* followed by any one of the consonants of the second column, completes the part of the word
that can precede its vowel.

The terms beyond the eighth show what comes after the
vowel. This portion is rather more complex than the beginning
of the word, and it would take too long to explain everything
in detail. The general principles of the symbolism will be
clear from the preceding explanations. The ninth term, with
its zero, denotes that a vowel can end the word if the vowel
is *a*—which means (1) the vowel of the article "a" and the
exclamation "huh?" and (2) the vowel of "pa," "ma," and
the exclamations "ah!" and "bah!"—or the vowel can end the
word if it is the *aw* sound, as in "paw," "thaw." In some dialects
(eastern New England, southern United States, South British)
the vowel ending occurs in words which are *spelled* with *ar*,
like "car," "star" (*ka, sta,* in these dialects), but in most of
the United States' dialects and in those of Ireland and Scot-
land these words end in an actual *r*. In eastern New England
and South British dialects, but not in southern United States,
these words cause a linking *r* to appear before a vowel beginning a following word. Thus for "far off" your Southerner says
fa of; your Bostonian and your Britisher say *fa rof,* with a liquid
initial *r;* but most of the United States says *far of,* with a rolled-
back *r*. For some dialects, term 9 would be different, showing
another possible final vowel, namely, the peculiar sound which
the Middle Westerner may notice in the Bostonian's pronunciation of "fur," "cur," (*fe, ke*) and no doubt may find very
queer. This funny sound is common in Welsh, Gaelic, Turkish,
Ute, and Hopi, but I am sure Boston did not get it from any of
these sources.

Can one-syllable words end in *e, i, o,* or *u?* No, not in English. The words so spelled end in a consonant sound, *y* or *w*.
Thus "I," when expressed in formula pattern, is *ay,* "we" is
wiy, "you" is *yuw,* "how" is *haw,* and so on. A comparison of
the Spanish *no* with the English "No!" shows that whereas the
Spanish word actually ends with its *o* sound trailing in the air,
the English equivalent closes upon a *w* sound. The patterns to
which we are habituated compel us to close upon a consonant

after most vowels. Hence when we learn Spanish, instead of saying *como no*, we are apt to say *kowmow now*; instead of *si*, we say our own word "see" (*siy*). In French, instead of *si beau*, we are apt to say "see bow."

Term 10 means that *r*, *w*, or *y* may be interpolated at this point except when the interpolation would result in joining *w* and *y* with each other. Term 11 means that the word may end in any single English consonant except *h*; this exception is most unlike some languages, e.g., Sanskrit, Arabic, Navaho, and Maya, in which many words end in *h*. The reader can figure out terms 12, 13, and 14 if he has stuck so far. A small *c* means *ch* as in "child"; *j* is as in "joy." Term 13, which contains these letters, expresses the possibility of words like "gulch," "bulge," "lunch," and "lounge." Term 14 represents the pattern of words like "health," "width," "eighth" (*eyt*θ), "sixth," "xth" (*eks*θ). Although we can say "nth" power or "fth" power, it takes effort to say the unpermitted "sth" power or "hth" power. "Hth" would be symbolized *eycθ, the star meaning that the form does not occur. Term 14, however, allows both *m*θ and *mpf*, the latter in words like "humph" or the recent "oomph" (*umpf*). The elements of term 15 may be added after anything—the *t* and *s* forms after voiceless sounds, the *d* and *z* after voiced sounds. Thus "towns" is *tawnz*, with *wnz* attained by term 10 plus 11 plus 15; whereas "bounce" is *bawns*, with *wns* by 10 plus 12. Some of the combinations resulting in this way are common; others are very rare but still are possible English forms. If Charlie McCarthy should pipe up in his coy way, "Thou oomphst, dost thou not?" or a Shakespearean actor should thunder out, "Thou triumphst!" the reason would be that the formula yields that weird sputter *mpfst* by term 14 plus term 15. Neither Mr. Bergen nor Mr. Shakespeare has any power to vary the formula.

The overriding factor applicable to the whole expression is a prohibition of doubling. Notwithstanding whatever the formula says, the same two consonants cannot be juxtaposed. While by term 15 we can add *t* to "flip" and get "flipt" ("flipped"), we can't add *t* to "hit" and get "hitt." Instead, at the point in the patterns where "hitt" might be expected we find simply "hit" (I hit it yesterday, I flipt it yesterday). Some languages, such as Arabic, have words like "hitt," "fadd," and so on, with both paired consonants distinct. The Creek Indian language permits three, e.g., nnn.

The way the patterns summarized in this formula control the forms of English words is really extraordinary. A new monosyllable turned out, say, by Walter Winchell or by a plugging ad man concocting a name for a new breakfast mush, is struck from this mold as surely as if I pulled the lever and the stamp came down on his brain. Thus linguistics, like the physical sciences, confers the power of prediction. I can predict, within limits, what Winchell will or won't do. He may coin a word "thrub," but he will not coin a word "srub," for the formula cannot produce an *sr*. A different formula indicates that if Winchell invents any word beginning with *th*, like "thell," or "therg," the *th* will have the sound it has in "thin," not the sound it has in "this" or "there." Winchell will not invent a word beginning with this latter sound.

We can wheeze forth the harshest successions of consonants if they are only according to the patterns producing the formula. We easily say "thirds" and "sixths," though "sixths" has the very rough sequence of four consonants, *ksθs*. But the simpler "sisths" is against the patterns and so is harder to say. "Glimpst" (glimpsed) has *gl* by term 3, *i* by 8, *mpst* by 12 plus 15. But "dlinpfk" is eliminated on several counts: Term 3 allows for no *dl*, and by no possible combination of terms can one get *npfk*. Yet the linguist can say "dlinpfk" as easily as he can say "glimpsed." The formula allows for no final *mb*; so we do not say "lamb" as it is spelled, but as *lam*. "Land," quite parallel but allowed by the formula, trips off our tongues as spelled. It is not hard to see why the "explanation," still found in some serious textbooks, that a language does this or that "for the sake of euphony" is on a par with nature's reputed abhorrence of a vacuum.

The exactness of this formula, typical of hundreds of others, shows that while linguistic formulations are not those of mathematics, they are nevertheless precise. We might bear in mind that this formula, compared with the formulation of some of the English (or other) grammatical patterns that deal with meaning, would appear like a simple sum in addition compared with a page of calculus. It is usually more convenient to treat very complex patterns by successive paragraphs of precise sentences and simpler formulas so arranged that each additional paragraph presupposes the previous ones, than to try to embrace all in one very complex formula.

MEANING IN LANGUAGE

PEOPLE can get into difficulties with language through ignorance of its mechanism. But the chief misuse of language stems from ignorance of the kinds of meaning that language conveys and from ignorance of the influence of language history.

SEMANTIC MEANING

The problem of meaning is one of the most difficult problems of psychology and philosophy. For our purposes, however, we may distinguish between two types of meaning: *semantic* and *syntactic*. Words that have semantic meaning refer to something outside of language. Thus *dog* and *justice* refer respectively to a type of observable object and to an "idea." On the other hand, words that have syntactic meaning serve only to indicate relationships in the language system, for example, *and*, *or*, etc.

In investigating semantic meaning the philosopher is often concerned with how words would be used if they were members of a perfectly formulated language. On the other hand, the linguist operates solely with language as it is used, the meanings normally or exceptionally attributed to each word, and the history of words. Thus the problems of semantic meaning for the linguist concern: (1) etymology, the history of words, and (2) lexicography, the meanings actually given to words.

The results of systematic study of word meanings are embodied in the modern dictionary. Let us look at the way a good student dictionary, such as *Webster's New World Dictionary*, gives the meanings of a simple word *child*:

> [ME. *childe*, pl. *childre* . . . AS. *cild*, pl. *cild*, *cildru*; akin to Goth. *kilthei*, womb; IE. **qel-t*, a swelling up < base **qel-*, rounded; sense development: rounded-swelling-womb-fetus-offspring; cf. CALF (animal)], 1. an infant; baby. 2. an unborn offspring. 3. a boy or girl in the period before puberty. 4. a son or daughter. 5. a descendant. 6. a person like a child in interests, judgment, etc., or regarded as a child; immature or childish adult. 7. a person regarded as the product of a specified place, time, etc.: as, a *child* of the Renaissance. 8. a thing that springs from a specified source; product: as, a *child* of one's imagination. . . .

The *World Webster* begins its account of this word, as with all others, with the etymology of the word, that is an analysis of the origin of the word and a history of changes in the word itself. This is followed by its lexicography, a list of the meanings of the word from its earliest surviving usage to its most recent usage. The etymology is enclosed in square brackets. First the history of the word in English is given by listing the Middle English (ME) and Anglo-Saxon (AS) forms. A word in a related language, Gothic (Goth.), follows. Then comes the derivation from the hypothetical base language, Indo-European (IE), from which many modern languages are presumed to be derived. The asterisk before such forms as **qel* indicates the hypothetical character of the word, that is, that such a word is not attested in documents, but is merely hypothecated on the basis of comparative study.

After the etymology appear the various meanings for the word *child*, arranged, as has been said, historically. Meanings 1 and 2, the earliest surviving meanings in English, are frequently employed. *Child* is used loosely to refer to a baby, and in "She is with child" to signify "unborn offspring." But perhaps most frequently we think of *child* in sense 3 as a person between babyhood and puberty. Meaning 3 is, of course, progressively developed from 1 and 2: foetal stage(2)>babyhood(1)>stage after babyhood(3). On the other hand, meanings 4 and 5 are differently oriented. They have reference not to a period of development in age, but to a relationship: son or daughter(4), descendant(5). Meaning 5 is exemplified in the expressions, "a child of the house of David," "children of Israel." When we use meaning 6, as in "He's nothing but a child," we refer to someone who *is not* a child in the sense of 3. We make use of metaphor. The grown person is like a child, not in age, but in personality or mental development. Meaning 6 thus suggests an attitude toward the person involved. Meanings 7 and 8 cannot be derived from meanings 3 or 6. "A child of misfortune," or "a child of the Middle Ages," has no connotations of age before puberty. Rather meanings 7 and 8 derive from meanings 4 and 5 (relationship). Persons living during the Middle Ages, or persons who are suffering misfortune may be thought of as descendants of the era or state of being: they have, so to speak, a family likeness.

The problem of semantic meaning is well illuminated by our study of the word *child,* which shows that: (1) *Meanings are complex.* (2) *Meanings,* like language itself, *are always changing.* (3) *Meanings convey both information and attitudes.*

(1) Meanings are complex. They are not merely variations of closely related concepts; in fact, they are frequently contradictory: *to dress beef* or *to dress a plank* means to shave off excess, whereas *to dress for a party* means to adorn or to put on articles of apparel not usually worn. Such differences are the cause of much ambiguity. For example, the phrase *a child of his age* can be interpreted in at least two distinct ways, one having to do with meaning 3, a person of a specific age between infancy and puberty, the other having to do with a period of history and probably referring to a grown person.

(2) Meanings are always changing. The different meanings of *child* were not given to it all at once. As time passed the original sense of the word was changed. The presumed Indo-

European root *qel which signified "rounded" first becomes
"swelling," which gives, in turn, the metaphoric idea of "womb."
The meaning of the word shifts to apply to what is contained in
the womb, "unborn child." For some cause, not easy to determine, the word meaning then shifts its temporal reference, becoming "infant," and "person between infancy and puberty."
Child takes on an additional meaning, differing from any pertaining to a period of development. The new connotation suggests relationship, "offspring." Metaphor once more comes into
play in "child of his age," "child of misfortune." In such ways
as this the meanings of the words in our vocabulary have
changed and continue to change.

The reasons for variation in meaning are difficult to discover.
In some cases the change seems to be due to certain social
influences. Thus *athlete*, a word borrowed from the Greek,
had an original meaning of "a competitor for a prize." But
today the basic meaning of the word is "anyone trained to
exercises of physical agility and strength." The only explanation for the change in meaning rests in the increased importance
of the athlete in modern society, particularly the professional
(and professional amateur). The athlete to us has become
someone to be admired for a special skill (lifting a weight,
hitting a ball or chin). But in many cases, as in *child*, there is
no adequate explanation for the change.

(3) Meanings convey both information and attitude. Saying
of a five-year-old, "He is a child," is different from saying the
same thing of an adult. Whereas the former statement simply
conveys *information*, the latter primarily conveys an *attitude*.

(a) Meaning as information. Because the writer whose chief
purpose is to convey information seeks to avoid meanings that
can arouse strong feelings, scientific and scholarly writing rarely
contains the kind of phrase that is found in political speeches
or tabloid newspapers. Although most words have meanings
which convey attitudes, the scholarly writer tries to use words
in such a way as to restrict their interpretation to the *neutral
level*, that is, the level of information. John Stuart Mill in the
following excerpt from his essay, *On Liberty*, is careful to avoid
words that will give rise to emotional meanings:

LOGIC AND LANGUAGE 74

> When there are persons to be found, who form an exception to the apparent unanimity of the world on any subject, even if the world is in the right, it is always probable that dissentients have something worth hearing to say for themselves, and that truth would lose something by their silence.

Mill uses no emotion-arousing words. Except for the almost unavoidable personification in *world*, his words point only to neutral meanings. He wishes to inform his audience, and thus convince them of the truth of what he is saying. He has deliberately forgone the attempt to appeal by use of provocative expressions. He could very easily have placed an adjective such as "self-reliant" before "persons," and replaced "dissentients" by an attitude-provoking word such as "thinking minority." His argument might have been "stronger," but it would have been less effective in view of Mill's scholarly purpose. Information can be given, of course, without restriction of words to neutral meanings. For example, popularizations of highly technical matters appear in the science sections of the New York *Times* or *Tribune*, although the vocabulary employed is more like that found in conversation than that in technical reports. But the emphasis is still on neutral rather than emotional meaning.

(b) Meaning as attitude. The attempt to avoid emotional responses to words is not so usual as the effort to secure such responses. The salesman does not merely want his client to agree that his product is good; he wants him to feel that he ought to buy it. He wishes to convey an attitude toward his product. The good teacher tries not only to give information, but also to convey an attitude toward his subject. The boy asking his father for the loan of his car wishes to get his father in the "right frame of mind." Perhaps the best way to show the contrast between meaning as information and meaning as attitude is to examine a skillful example of "persuasive" writing. Milton in his *Areopagitica* writes not only to show that freedom of the press is advantageous, but also to persuade us to act to secure this freedom. A sentence from

Milton's discussion of the relationship between virtue and freedom will serve as illustration:

> I cannot praise a fugitive and cloistered virtue unexercised and unbreathed, that never sallies out and sees her adversary, but slinks out of the race, where that immortal garland is to be run for, not without dust and heat.

His point is that a man can become virtuous only by knowing the good and the bad. Since the press plays a vital role in supplying mankind with information, society should not condone censorship.

Notice how Milton gets his effects. The whole sentence is built upon metaphor, and by this means Milton makes the reader visualize virtue as a race to be won. Instead of a neutral statement about the difficulties of attaining a virtuous life, Milton speaks of an "immortal garland" to be won in the "dust and heat." Instead of saying that evil must be met, not merely be avoided, he metaphorically contrasts the "cloister" and a "hot, dusty road." In almost all the key words he avoids the neutral level of meaning in favor of the metaphoric ones. The images serve to give the reader the emotional reaction that would not be present in a strictly neutral presentation.

Persuasion is not the only function served by language usage which relies heavily upon the metaphoric level of meaning. Imagery is also the stock in trade of poetry and the novel. But, whereas in persuasion the images serve to create active belief, in poetry and the novel the images serve to create vivid impressions. Thus Dickens begins his *Bleak House* with a picture of the fog: he does this not to give information about a natural phenomenon, nor to make the reader want to crusade against fog; rather, he wishes to create a mood appropriate to the somber events of his story:

> Fog everywhere. Fog up the river, where it flows among green aits and meadows; fog down the river, where it rolls defiled among the tiers of shipping, and the waterside pollu-

tions of a great (and dirty) city. Fog on the Essex marshes, fog on the Kentish heights. Fog creeping into the cabooses of collier-brigs, fog lying out on the yards, and hovering in the rigging of great ships; fog drooping on the gunwales of barges and small boats. Fog in the eyes and throats of ancient Greenwich pensioners, wheezing by the firesides of their wards; fog in the stem and bowl of the afternoon pipe of the wrathful skipper, down in his close cabin; fog cruelly pinching the toes and fingers of his shivering little 'prentice boy on deck. Chance people on the bridges peeping over the parapets into a nether sky of fog, with fog all round them, as if they were up in a balloon, and hanging in the misty clouds.

His description of fog over a river not only gives an objective account of an occurrence, but it also conveys the ghostly effect that accompanies the presence of fog. His imagery makes the reader part of the scene Dickens is describing and part of the mood. Dickens's highly metaphoric word choice, when compared with that of Mill, suggests how wide is the range of effects that can be achieved by the manipulation of the semantic meaning of words.

SYNTACTIC MEANING

As we have seen, constant repetition of speech patterns makes their use automatic and "natural," so that a person speaking English would think it strange to hear someone say, "Raining it will be today," instead of "It will be raining today." He expects to use certain patterns of speech, and is usually so much controlled by them that he might well consider "Rain it will today" much stranger than the combination of words in the nonsense passage by Sam Clemens cited above, perhaps stranger even than the poem *Jabberwocky*. In the former, all the words are recognizable and fit into acceptable patterns; in the latter, even though most of the words are not recognizable, they at least fall into acceptable patterns.

How speech habits are controlled by a feeling for patterns

is illustrated by the "mistakes" that children make when they are still unsure of their language. "Daddy, it's funner at the beach with you," or, "Daddy, we goed there yesterday" are not random creations. The child is simply relying upon a normal pattern in these "mistakes," that is, upon the usual comparative with *-er* and the usual past with *-ed*. His responses are governed by analogy with patterns he has already learned, almost as in an equation:

nice: nicer = fun: funner
walk: walked = go: goed

These patterns make up *syntactic meaning* in language. Obviously in any statement, part of it is concerned with the pattern of speech, with meaning that has reference only to the statement itself, not to any external event, as with semantic meaning. Syntactic meaning is best illustrated by comparing such words as *a, and, of* with a word such as *dog*. The latter refers to an external object, the former do not.

To express syntactic meaning, language has three primary resources: (1) order, (2) formal change, and (3) use of function words.

(1) *Order*. Syntactic meaning may be expressed by the order of elements in a sentence. In "Boy loves girl" the subject and object of the sentence are indicated simply by position. In the following examples all the words remain unchanged; word order is the chief means for indicating syntactic meaning (subject, verb, object, etc.): Keep the home fires burning: Fires keep the home burning: Keep fires burning the home: Keep home the burning fires. Curiously enough English in its reliance upon word order is closer to such a language as Chinese than it is to its own historical origins, for English in the beginning relied upon formal change.

(2) *Formal change*. A language such as Latin (and in the beginning English) expresses syntactic meaning chiefly by means of phonetic modification and alteration, that is, formal change. The Latin sentence, *"Puer amat puellam,"* means "Boy (*puer*) loves (*amat*) girl (*puellam*)." But change in word order makes no difference in syntactic meaning: both *"Puer amat puellam"*

and "*Puellam amat puer*" mean "Boy loves girl." The absence of an ending on *puer* indicates that it is the subject; the *am* added to *puell* indicates object; the *at* added to *am* indicates the verb, present tense, agreeing with a third person, singular subject.

Although Modern English, as we have seen, depends chiefly upon word order to indicate syntactic meaning, the earliest form of English, Anglo-Saxon, is a so-called *inflected* language, that is, one which employs formal change as its primary means for indicating syntactic meaning. This may be illustrated by comparing the Modern English adjective *green* with its Anglo-Saxon ancestor. In Modern English the positive form of the adjective *green* never changes. In Anglo-Saxon the adjective has gender (as in Latin, French, etc.), and two systems of inflectional endings, depending upon the presence or absence of the article; to illustrate there follows one of the two types of inflections of Anglo-Saxon *grēne* in the singular:

	Masculine	*Neuter*	*Feminine*
Nominative	grēne	grēne	grēnu
Genitive	grēnes	grēnes	grēnre
Dative	grēnum	grēnum	grēnre
Accusative	grēnne	grēne	grēne
Instrumental	grēne	grēne	

Similar employment of formal change is found in the verb and noun. The clearest vestiges of the Anglo-Saxon system in Modern English are the -*s* plural of nouns and the dual system of indicating change in tense in the verb. In Anglo-Saxon, verbs were of two types, one indicating tense by alteration of the vowel in the stem; the other by use of endings:

Type One

INFINITIVE	PAST SINGULAR	PAST PLURAL	PAST PARTICIPLE
bīdan	bād	bidon	biden (await)
bēodan	bēad	budon	boden (command)

Type Two

fremman	fremede	fremedon	fremed (perform)

Similarly in Modern English two verb types appear:

Type One

sing   sang   sang   sung

Type Two

change   changed   changed   changed

It should be noted that the drift toward reliance upon word order is already perceptible in Anglo-Saxon, a drift which has transformed the basic syntactic structure of English.

A subsidiary type of formal change involving pitch and stress is also employed in Modern English. *Pitch* is used, for example, to mark the end of a sentence. When a statement has been completed, the pitch lowers; when a statement is made requiring an answer, the pitch rises. *Stress* is used in English to secure emphasis, to mark word units, and to indicate whether words are being used as verbs or nouns: 're bel re 'bel; 'con vert con 'vert; 'di gest di 'gest.

(3) *Function words.* A third method of showing syntactic relations, found in all languages, involves the use of function words. English makes complicated verbal distinctions by using function words (auxiliaries), as in the following italicized examples: *is* going, *has* gone, *had* gone, *may* go, *does* go, etc. Other function words, prepositions (of, in, on, etc.) and conjunctions (and, or, where, etc.), serve to link together sentence elements: "Mary *and* (conj.) John went *to* (prep.) the movies, *but* (conj.) Joe stayed *where* (conj.) he was." Finally the function words *the* and *a* (articles) indicate whether we are talking about a specific person, "*the* boy," or of a specific example of a type, "*a* boy." Consider the number of function words and the very refined shades of meaning conveyed in the following:

> Next week he goes *to* Chicago where he *may* stay two days, *as* he *did* last year. He *will* leave *for* Detroit *before the* end *of a* week. *Then* he *is* going *to* Buffalo. He *must* go *to* Albany *and should* go *to* Troy. He *will* go *to* New York, *if* he *is* able. He *will have* gone *over* three thousand miles.

Thus these three methods of indicating syntactic meaning—order, formal change, and use of function words—are all employed in Modern English. As we have seen, formal change was originally of chief importance in English. Nouns could be clearly distinguished from verbs by their inflectional endings; all the parts of speech were distinct in form. But in Modern English formal change is of far less importance than word order and the use of function words in distinguishing "parts of speech." In fact, it is often difficult to identify the part of speech of a word merely from its form. Consider the word *light* as it is used in the following sentences: The light is in the room; Light the room; The room is light; He traveled light. Although the form of the word remains unchanged, it is respectively noun, verb, adjective, adverb. We can classify it only in relation to its position in the sentence (word order) and in relation to the function words employed. The sentence, "Boy loves girl," illustrates the importance of word order in English. Newspaper headlines supply many illustrations of the importance of employing and properly placing function words. Thus the syntactic ambiguity of the headline, "Truman reports open meeting," can be resolved simply by placing the function word *an* before *open* or the function word *the* before *meeting*.

With the knowledge that meaning is both syntactic and semantic, a more precise reason for Alice's confusion over the *Jabberwocky* (see Chapter 2) can now be given. Not only were the phonemes all combined in acceptable arrangements, but also there was a syntactic pattern that corresponded to the kind of syntactic patterns found when English is used meaningfully. For example, the function words *and, all, were, the* were all in their proper places. Even the word *outgrabe* seems to be the past tense of some word such as *outgribe*. Indeed the syntactic patterns of the first verse of the *Jabberwocky* may be isolated by blocking out all units of possible semantic reference:

> 'Twas . . . . . ig and the . . . . . y . . . . s
> Did . . . . and . . . in the . . . . :
> All . . . . y were the . . . . s,
> And the . . . . s . . . . a . . . .

There is a familiar syntactic pattern here. But syntactic meaning is no guarantee of the presence of semantic meaning.

Our automatic response to syntactic patterns is ingrained in us at an early age. As a result we tend to insert all words into the same familiar patterns. Note, for example, how without any thought we can fit new concepts into old patterns. When the telegraph was invented, we first made a new name out of old materials, borrowed from the Greek, and then with no difficulty substituted the strange new word in an old formula. Instead of "I sent a message," we say, "I sent a telegram." On the other hand, our habit of responding only to specific types of language patterns makes us reject variations in syntactic structure. We accept statements of the form "All redheads are irritable," and "All metals are malleable," but not of the form "Redheads irritable are all," or "Malleable all are metals." Only a statement which conforms to acceptable patterns will be recognized as a statement in the English language.

The habit of responding readily to patterns which are part of the structure of language sometimes has the unfortunate effect of making sentences with similar sentence structure appear equally acceptable. It tends to obscure the real difference between the statement "All redheads are irritable" and "All metals are malleable." Because they have the same standard pattern, we can be misled into thinking they have the same truth value. But it should be apparent at the outset that one statement is reliable, the other is not. Here is perhaps one of the reasons why we are so ready to jump to conclusions and to make snap judgments. Our reliance upon language tends to make us forget that a grammatically correct statement can be very unreliable.

Similarly habits of language sometimes prevent us from seeing the difference between statements such as "World government will take away personal freedom" and "All tyrannies will take away personal freedom." Ordinary English usage insufficiently distinguishes between an existent, verifiable subject (tyranny) and a nonexistent, non-verifiable subject (world government). We can make reliable predictions, as we shall see in Chapter Five, based upon past experience with existent subjects. But when we argue as if a nonexistent subject, for example, world government, exists because we have used it as the subject of a sentence, we mistake syntactic correctness for truth.

Finally it is important to recognize that syntactic patterns are anything but inert. They may be manipulated—as sounds and meanings may be manipulated—in order to help create attitudes. The quotation from Milton's *Areopagitica* is a good example of such manipulation:

> I cannot praise a fugitive and cloistered virtue unexercised and unbreathed, that never sallies out and sees her adversary, but slinks out of the race, where that immortal garland is to be run for, not without dust and heat.

Note how the variations in the syntactic patterns add to the effectiveness of the sentence. 1) Balance or parallelism is employed in the repetition of compound phrases: fugitive *and* cloistered, unexercised *and* unbreathed, sallies out *and* sees, dust *and* heat. 2) Periodic structure is used; that is, the meaning of the sentence is not complete until the last phrase, "dust and heat." Milton's main point is that the "immortal garland" of real virtue is attained only when virtue is tested by trial, i.e., "dust and heat." Closely allied to the effect produced by syntactic manipulation is the effect produced by Milton's use of sound patterns. He employs alliteration, repetition of the same initial sound in a series of words, as in *s*allies, *s*ees, *s*links; *r*ace, *r*un; he uses initial rhymes, *un*exercised, *un*breathed. He constructs an elaborate pattern in his repetitive use of sibilants: cloistered, unexercised, sallies, sees, adversary, slinks, and in his variation of vowel sounds as in sallies, sees, slinks. Thus sound and syntax can combine to reinforce strongly the effect of attitude-producing words.

LANGUAGE HISTORY: SOCIETY AND THE INDIVIDUAL

Dictionary definitions rely heavily upon the explanatory force of language history, and, as we have seen, Modern English syntax can be understood only with some knowledge of earlier periods of the language. Obviously some knowledge of the principles of language history is necessary to an understanding of meaning in language.

Language, like all social institutions such as law and government, results from men living together in a social group. In consequence language, like the other social institutions, has a history. It is not remade by each generation; rather each succeeding generation accepts and modifies the language of the preceding generation. Although no lawyer would act without knowing something of the history of the law, most of us use language, even at critical junctures, without awareness of the burden of history that every language statement carries. Language exists as a result of the operation of complex forces of the past modified by present needs. If we are not aware of this, we are particularly insensitive to the full implications of much that we speak and hear.

Although the speech of a preceding generation is modified by the succeeding one, the modification is so slight as to be almost imperceptible. For this reason each age is able to understand the preceding one. Difficulties occur only after several generations have each in turn modified a language. Thus the English of the nineteenth century can be read without difficulty, whereas the language of Chaucer, Middle English, seems to need translation:

> Ye knowe ek, that in form of speche is chaunge
> Withinne a thousand yeer, and wordes tho
> That hadden pris, now wonder nyce and straunge
> Us thinketh hem, and yet thei spake hem so . . .
>   (from *Troilus and Criseyde*)

Translation:

You know too that in the form of speech there is change during a thousand years, and words then that were valued, now wonderfully peculiar and strange they seem to us—and yet they spoke them thus.

The sounds of words have changed; syntactic structure is somewhat different; words have changed their meaning, been lost, and new words have appeared.

The specific reasons for changes in language have proved difficult to discover. But linguists have suggested several possibilities. Changes may be due to individual error or ingenuity.
Lapses, that is, unconscious variations from a normal pattern,
occur frequently. The current use of the word *normalcy* is usually traced to a lapse by President Harding who used the word
in happy ignorance of the accepted form *normality*. We laugh
at such slips as *Flederic* for *Frederic* or *comferable* for *comfort-
able*. Yet lapses occur constantly in ordinary speech. Not even
the most highly trained speaker can completely avoid them.
Similarly, people are constantly using the "wrong" word:
"When called upon unexpectedly President Eisenhower spoke
extraneously," "He looked as if he were getting better, but com-
plexes set in." When the speaker is aware of his blunder, he
will correct himself because he realizes that he has not used
the "right" word, the one which the social group has decreed is
appropriate. The effect of the individual upon the vocabulary
of language may also be observed in the deliberate creation of
new words. Thus Walter Winchell created the new word *debu-
tramp* and Lewis Carroll the word *chortle* from *snort* and
chuckle. Words of this type, which may at first seem strange, if
they are used with any frequency gradually become accepted.

Another possible cause of change is the historical drift which
seems to operate upon sounds in all languages. Because of this
drift, sounds in a language tend to be modified according to a
regular pattern. This fact makes possible descriptive laws of
sound change. For example, the long vowels have changed historically in English according to a regular pattern.

Old English (*Anglo-Saxon*)	*Old English Pronunciation* (approximate)	*Modern English*
ath		oath
ban		bone
bat	ā as in *father*	boat
gat		goat
ham		home

sae		sea
waed	$\bar{a}e$ = e in *met*	weed
claene		clean
cwen		queen
fedan	$\bar{e}$ = a in *sane*	feed
me		me
cniht		knight
niht	$\bar{i}$ = ee in *meet*	night
mine		mine
gos		goose
col	$\bar{o}$ as in *note*	cool
hrof		roof
ut		out
hus	$\bar{u}$ as in *lute*	house
mus		mouse

This regularity of sound change, which can be illustrated from any language, provided the linguist with his best tool for studying the historical development of the modern languages. Armed with the knowledge that sound changes are regular, linguists succeeded in showing the family relations of language after language. Of particular importance for English was the discovery that many modern languages, including English, presumably developed, as shown in the chart (p. 86), from an original, lost language called Indo-European.

The establishment of this language family was one of the important discoveries of the nineteenth century. At one time the biblical story of the Tower of Babel suggested to language students either the uselessness of the comparative study of language or it seemed to point to Hebrew (a Semitic language) as the parent language. Then European students of Sanskrit noted a series of correspondences between words in Sanskrit, Greek, and Latin, for example, the words for father and mother.

Sanskrit	Latin	Greek
pitár	pater	patér
matr	mater	mater

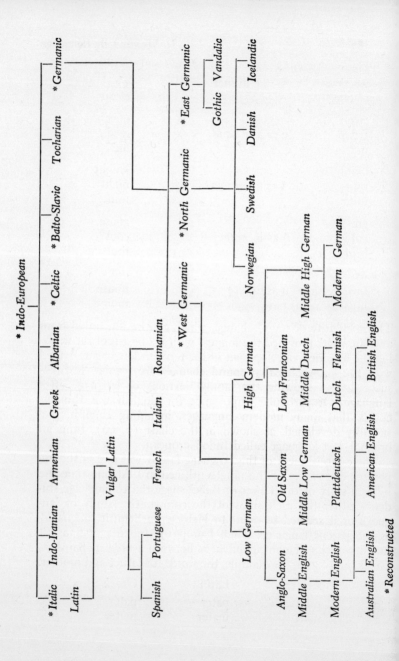

* Reconstructed

It became apparent that the correspondences could not be fortuitous. At the same time investigation of other European languages revealed similarities that could be explained only by the hypothesis of a parent Indo-European language. For example, the words *three* and *mother* are so alike in the various languages studied that they almost certainly must have been derived from a common origin. It is conjectured that the Indo-European word for three was **treyes* and for mother, **matr*.

Language	Words	
English	three	mother
Dutch	drie	moeder
Flemish	drie	moeder
German	drei	mutter
Icelandic	thrja	mothir
Swedish	tre	moder
Danish	tre	mor
Norwegian	tre	mor
Latin	tres	mater
French	trois	mère
Spanish	tres	madre
Portuguese	tres	mae
Italian	tre	madre
Roumanian	trei	mama
Czech	tri	matko
Polish	trzy	matko
Russian	tri	matj
Bulgarian	tri	maika
Irish	tri	mathain
Greek	treis	mater
Sanskrit	tri	matr

Similarly, the Danish scholar Rask and the German scholar Grimm from detailed comparative study established the hypothesis that a shift had taken place in certain initial consonants in parent Germanic: thus Indo-European initial *p* appears as Germanic *f*, Latin *piscis* = English *fish*, Latin *ped-is* = English *foot*. A "law" governing the Germanic consonant shift was established. One part of the law establishes the following correspondences (the law is actually more extensive and also covers consonants in other than initial position):

I.E.		Ger.		I.E.		Ger.
b	>	p		p	>	f
d	>	t		t	>	th
g	>	k		k	>	h

An illustration of the operation of the Germanic consonant shift is given in the chart (p. 89).

On the other hand, social pressures have a great deal to do with the formation of the vocabulary of a language. This may be illustrated by a glance at the development of the English vocabulary. The Germanic invaders who brought the language that was to become English to England were a barbaric, pagan people. Yet even a fringe of contact with Rome had influenced their culture before their conquest of England. This is evidenced in the fact that they brought with them certain words including

cheap	<	caupo
-chester	<	castra
street	<	strata
tile	<	tegula
wall	<	vallum
wine	<	vinum

By the seventh century the Anglo-Saxons were converted to Christianity and developed a civilization which gave England an important place in Western Christendom. Again the English vocabulary shows evidence of extensive borrowing from Latin, for example, words like *alms, disciple, mass,* etc. Because Anglo-Saxon tended to enlarge its vocabulary by word building, using its native resources, it tended to resist borrowings. Thus the full influence of Latin can be seen only when we take into account

English	Germanic	Celtic	Latin	Greek	Balto-Slavic	Indo-Iranian
apple	apfel	ubull	abella		jábloko	
peg		bacc	baculum	baktron	bāksteleti	
ten	zehn	dek	decem	deka	dëšimt	daśa
two	zwei	dou	duo	dyo	du	dua
tree	treue	druid	durus	dóru	dé revo	daru
kin	kint		genus	genos		janah
cold	kalt	—gint	gelu	gelandron		
acre	acker		ager	agros		ajra-h
father	vater		pater	patér		pitár
foot	fuss		pedis	pos		
fee			pecu			
thin	dünn		tenuis	teino		
hore (A.S.)			carus			

English words which are actually translations of the Latin, such as *godspel* (gospel), a translation of *bonus nuntius*, made by compounding two native words *god* (good) and *spel* (word). Similarly, *almigtig* (almighty) translated *omnipotens*.

A further influence upon the vocabulary of the English language, which clearly reveals the pressure of social change, may be perceived before the end of the Old English period. As a result of the Viking invasions of the ninth and tenth centuries England was partitioned, with the north being settled by Scandinavian peoples, speaking a language sufficiently close to English, so that communication between the neighboring people was apparently possible. At any rate, proximity resulted in Scandinavian influencing English in its basic vocabulary, as in the following: *anger, big, bull, cake, fellow, ill, leg, sly, ugly*. Scandinavian borrowings appear even in many function words, which because of their syntactic function are least amenable to change. Thus, *till, though, same, both, they, their, them* are all Scandinavian.

The most dramatic influence upon English, however, resulted from the Norman Conquest of 1066. For three centuries following the Conquest England was ruled by a French-speaking nobility. But English proved too hardy to succumb. It remained the language spoken by most Englishmen, and its written form shows an unbroken line of continuity. By the fourteenth century English had conquered its conquerors; it again became the recognized language of government and of law courts; it was the language used by Chaucer. But its "underground" existence had a great effect upon its vocabulary and its syntax. Thus the tendency toward reliance on word order instead of formal change was strengthened after the Conquest, perhaps because English under the Normans was not a "school" language and was not written very much. At any rate, English emerged in the fourteenth century primarily dependent upon word order and upon the use of function words.

The English vocabulary was greatly enlarged and greatly modified. So extensive is this borrowing that no list of words would suffice to illustrate. But a glance at the etymologies on almost any page of the dictionary will suggest how much of our vocabulary is French. Whereas the Anglo-Saxons extended native words through composition and derivation, their descendants learned to borrow new words. Obviously the social determinant in this change of habit was the dominating influence of French. In order to survive, English had to adapt itself to the ways of the conqueror; it did this by assimilating a vast store of French words. Thereafter people speaking English learned to combine French, Latin, and English elements without any feeling of strangeness.

The new habit of assimilation resulted in English developing a vast store of words which have almost dwarfed its original Anglo-Saxon word hoard. In its borrowing of foreign words our English vocabulary reflects some of the great historical movements of modern history. Thus, during the Renaissance in England, English began to replace Latin as the primary language of science and learning. At the same time Latin remained the revered language of scholars. The result of the complex of new habits of assimilation, of the use of English in learning, and of the reverence for Latin was to enlarge the English vocabulary with great numbers of Latin borrowings, again best exemplified by a random glance at the etymologies in a dictionary. The industrial and scientific revolutions of modern times are reflected in our vocabulary by numbers of borrowings from Latin, *radio, transmitter, continuum, nucleus,* etc.; and from Greek particularly, *telephone, telegraph, photograph, phonetics, phylogeny,* etc. The spread of English throughout the world is similarly reflected in the number of borrowings from the languages of distant lands: *zebra* (Portuguese from West African), *gong* (Maylay), *sash* (Arabic), *taboo* (Polynesian), *canoe* (American Indian).

Finally, changes in social institutions are clearly reflected in language. The invention of the telephone and telegraph not only introduced these words, but also occupational words such as *linesman, telegrapher, switchboard operator, telephone repairman,* etc. Conversely, the decline of institutions led to the loss from the active vocabulary of words pertaining to the institution. Thus when feudalism declined many occupational words were lost, words such as *reeve, vassal, franklin,* etc.

Language, it is clear, undergoes change because of individual intervention, but chiefly as the result of the interplay of large social forces. Language is given man by the society in which he lives. At the same time, it is an aggregate of the speech of individuals, so that in varying degrees each individual modifies the language he speaks. Sometimes a great poet or a great thinker has had a lasting and appreciable effect upon the language. On the other hand, for most of us it is a passive and mechanical thing used to fulfill certain needs and wants. We rarely endeavor to add to the language or even to use it efficiently and effectively.

Obviously we could not use language effectively if we were to pay too much attention to it; it is, after all, a means, not an end in itself. Yet the accumulation of an enormous fund of English words has made English complex and, in consequence, difficult to use with maximum efficiency. Words have become so overburdened with meanings that the simplest sentence can be ambiguous. Writers must frequently spend more time explaining their words than analyzing specific problems. Thus some awareness of the complexities of meaning in language and language history is necessary if we are to make language a sensitive instrument, one that we can use effectively and efficiently. One simple way to become acquainted with words is to get the most out of the dictionary. Instead of simply looking up a word to "get its meaning," read and study the etymologies and the definitions, as was done earlier in this chapter with the word *child*. To be ignorant of the resources, the history, the dangers of language is like traveling without brakes on a busy highway.

EXERCISES

1. *Each of the following articles has to do with a language "problem." Analyze and discuss each in the light of this chapter.*

(a) *"Insuperable Pidgin?" from* Time,[1] *August 10, 1953.* Half a century had passed since the white men first sounded

[1] Articles (a), (b), (c), and (d) are reprinted by permission of *Time* Magazine; copyright Time Inc. 1953.

the warning. "This Pidgin nonsense," cried the globe-trotting Baron von Hesse-Wartegg, should be replaced "by a sensible German language." But in spite of the baron—and all the efforts of imperial German officials—the natives of the New Guinea protectorate went right on speaking Pidgin, the language built up from years of dealing with white traders. By World War II, G.I.s were being taught to say: *"Cut-im grass belong head belong me"* ("I want a haircut"), and the 23rd Psalm was still going native in a wide variety of ways: e.g., Australia's *"Big Name watchem sheepysheep. Watchum blackfella. No more belly cry fella hab . . ."*; New Guinea's *"Deus iwas gut long mi, im igifim mi ol samtig. . . ."*

Last week the old battle was raging again. The U.N.'s Trusteeship Council noted that Pidgin "has characteristics . . . which reflect now outmoded concepts of the relationship between indigenous inhabitants and immigrant groups" (U.N. Pidgin for "It's undemocratic"). The council's recommendation: that New Guinea's Australian administrators "develop plans to eliminate [Pidgin] completely." Would the resolution do the trick? Cried Paul Hasluck, Australia's Minister for Territories: "Just as foolish as suggesting that all Europeans should speak nothing but Russian next week."

Added the Sydney *Morning Herald:* "If 50 years ago the Germans found it impossible to defeat the spread of Pidgin . . . the problem now facing Australia is insuperable. The simple fact, of course, is that . . . Pidgin English has become a language in its own right, and no matter how many pious sentiments are expressed in the U.N. or elsewhere, its use and continued spread cannot be curbed." In other words, no matter how much busybody *ol man bilong ples longwey* (foreigners) fuss and fume, *ol man bilong Nugini* will go right on making *toktok* as they please.

Do you consider the writer's conclusion to be reliable? Explain.

(b) *"How to Be Amika," from* Time, *July 27, 1953.*

Charles Thollet, a hardware dealer of Port-Lyautey, French Morocco, knows only a little English, but that did not bother him when he planned a trip through the U.S. He only looked up some addresses, and sent off a few letters beginning *"Estimata Sinjoro."* Last week the "Dear Sirs" of the U.S. were entertaining him and his wife royally. The language they used: Esperanto.

In the 66 years since Polish Physician Lazarus Ludwig Zamenhof invented it, Esperanto has not become the world language he hoped for, but it has turned into a minor international cult. Today, Esperantists claim to be 1,500,000 strong, about 10,000 of them in the U.S. There are Esperanto books from *La Sankta Biblio* to *Kiel Placas Al Vi* (*As You Like It*). Australia has made a movie in it; KLM has advertised, *"Flugado sparas tempon kaj monon"* (Flying saves time and money); Bing Crosby sang an Esperanto song in *The Road to Singapore*. Last week the Thollets proved what tourists can accomplish by simply asking, *"Cu vi parolas Esperante?"*

A mild-mannered little man who learned the language in three months, Charles Thollet, got his first taste of American hospitality when he received a shore-to-ship telephone call while still one day out of New York: *"Vi estas bonvenita en Usono."* Next day a group of enthusiastic Esperantists were at the pier. They whisked the Thollets through customs, drove them to a hotel, took them up the Empire State Building (*"Kiel alta!"* exclaimed the Thollets), wined and dined them for six days.

In Detroit, another group of Esperantists took them through the Ford plant (*"Kiel granda!"*), and in Chicago, still another group showed them the stockyards (*"Kiel multaj bestoj!"*). Last week, back in Manhattan after a visit with California Esperantists and a few days in Washington, D. C., the Thollets happily pronounced the U.S. *"pura, agrabla, kaj automata."* But above all, they said, it is *amika* (friendly). Added *Sinjoro* Thollet to a reporter: "You ought to learn Esperanto. Only three months. *Tiel facila!"*

Would you agree that Esperanto (or any "universal" language) will solve the problem of international cooperation? Discuss in relation to (a) and to Exercise 2a in Chapter 2.

(c) *"Going to the Point" from* Time, November 9, 1953.

West Point's entrance exams are still months away, but many a would-be cadet is already worrying about how he should prepare. Last week the worriers could get some help from a book called *How to Pass Annapolis and West Point Entrance Exams* (Arco: $3.50). Judging by the book's sample questions, candidates would find that the Point expects from every man quite a lot.

The tests cover everything from trapezoids to Tom Paine, from spelling (*acquiesence, acquiescence, aquiescence, acquiesance*) to literature ("What Joseph Lincoln did for Cape Cod, Sarah Orne Jewett did for 1) Florida, 2) Maine, 3) Oregon, 4) Michigan"). But just knowing the usual subjects is far from enough. To test their intelligence, the Point also presents candidates with a whole new bogus language that changes from year to year.

To start off, the candidates must master a mock set of rules. In Arco's example of an artificial-language, plurals end in *s*, numerals must follow nouns, and *kim, kima, kime, kimi* mean who, whose, to whom, and whom. Candidates must then use the rules to count (*bal* is one, *bals* is ten, *balsebal* is eleven, etc.) and to conjugate verbs (*binob*, I am; *binol*, you are; *binom*, he is; *binof*, she is; *binos*, it is; *binobs*, we are; *binols*, you are; *binoms*, they are).

After that, here are a few instructions about gender (if *jeval* is horse, *omjeval* is stallion and *jijeval* is mare, ordinal numbers (*balid* is first, *balsid* is tenth), and adjectives (add *ik* to noun stems). Finally there are a hundred words of vocabulary. Samples:

> I live—lodob
> book—buk
> teacher—tidel
> one who—ut
> wine—vin
> I—ob

author—lautel
I drink—dlinob
I have—labob
you—ol
woman—vom
I write—penob
this—at
two—tel
house—dom
four—fol
man—man
and—e
scholar—julel

With all that in mind, says Arco, any future cadet should have no trouble at all translating the following:

Vom dlinof vini. Buk at binom olik. Tidel obsik labom julelis. Tidel obsik labom, julelis telsefol. Man ut, kel lodom in dom, binom lautel, e penom bukis.[2]

1) What is the basis for the inclusion of such a question in the entrance examination? Do you think it is a good question? Explain.
2) Try to set up the rudiments of another artificial language.

(d) "The Lost Positive," from Time, September 21, 1953.

I know a little man both ept and ert.
And intro? extro? No, he's just a vert.
Sheveled and couth and kempt, pecunious, ane;
His image trudes upon the ceptive brain.

Rhymester David McCord is fascinated by what happened to the positive form of such common words as inept, inert, disheveled, uncouth and unkempt. For years, McCord, who is secretary of the Alumni Fund of Harvard University and a well-known writer of light verse, has waged a happy campaign for

[2] Translation: The woman drinks wine. This book is yours. Our teacher has 24 scholars. The man who lives in that house is an author and writes books.

the restoration of what he calls the Lost Positive. For amusement he writes sprightly rhymes full of positives, like the one above (which he calls *Gloss*) published in the January *Harper's Magazine.*

Last week it looked as if McCord's campaign was getting somewhere. New York *Herald Tribune* Columnist John Crosby had "dorsed" the trend, proclaimed himself a member of the "Society for the Restoration of Lost Positives." Later, a smart copywriter for Gimbel's picked up the idea, blazoned an eight-column ad for fall college fashions: "couth, kempt, sheveled . . . that's how college girls will look this fall."

But McCord was already ahead of them. Cloistered in his Harvard office, he was busy turning out more Lost Positives: *licit, iterate, fulgent, prentice, placable, delible, souciant, effable, vertently, fangled, sponsible, pression, fatigable.* McCord says he prefers real Lost Positives, but for fun sometimes uses false ones, such as *pistle.* "The prefix in that word is really not the Latin *e* but the Greek *epi,*" he explains. This justified his reply to a friend who sent him a clipping with a note: "Lighted to ward the closed which is cised from days *Irish Times.*" McCord wrote back: "Pistle ceived and tents gladly noted."

McCord even got around to another Lost Positive verse which begins:

> Some day, full of ertia,
> I'll be taking off for Persia.

1) What general principle of language helps to explain the phenomenon of the "lost positive"?
2) Try to explain in detail why some of the words given have no positive.

(e) *"How to Spot a Communist," from* New York Times, *Sunday, June 12, 1955.*

The American Civil Liberties Union asked Secretary of Defense Charles E. Wilson yesterday to withdraw a pamphlet, "How to Spot a Communist." The publication was prepared by the First Army and used by the Watertown, Mass., Arsenal of the Ordnance Corps and the Continental Air Command.

The Liberties Union attacked it as a "serious threat to free thought and expression."

According to the A.C.L.U., the pamphlet lists certain words, associations and views as clues or "danger signals indicating Communist beliefs."

In a letter to Mr. Wilson, Ernest Angell, chairman, and Patrick Murphy Malin, executive director of the union, declared: "There is little doubt that the publication in question, despite its disavowal that none of these criteria are proof of Communist support, can spur citizens to spy on one another's language, expressions and associations."

Among the "clues" listed by the pamphlet are such words as "vanguard," "colonialism," "chauvinism," "book-burning," "demagogy," "witch-hunt," "dialectical," "reactionary," "exploitation," "materialist" and "progressive."

Other "clues" include "specific issues [that] have been in the Communist arsenal for a long period of time." These include "McCarthyism," "violation of civil rights," "racial or religious discrimination," "immigration laws," "anti-subversive legislation," "any legislation concerning labor unions," "the military budget" and "peace."

With respect to "associations" the pamphlet says: "Generally speaking, it is well to be wary of those organizations which stand for wholesale condemnation of the United States Government, a legitimate political party or groups of individuals. Communist fronts have consistently shown preference for such issues as 'civil rights,' 'anti-subversive legislation' and 'restrictions on immigration.'

"In addition these groups frequently seize on any controversial subject from fluoridation of drinking water to 'police brutality' in order to promote their nefarious schemes."

The A.C.L.U. letter to Secretary Wilson asserted that words designated by the pamphlet as "danger signals" are "frequently used by non-Communists and even anti-Communists . . . and by Administration spokesmen in speeches attacking the Communist conspiracy."

From what has been said in the chapter, do you consider the objections to the pamphlet to be valid? Explain.

(*f*) *"Independence Unit Unusual as It Backs Major Party Man," by Robert McManus, from* Binghamton Press, *October 4, 1953.*

Major Donald W. Kramer's Independence Party occupied the political spotlight in Binghamton last week. Independent parties have different purposes under different circumstances. Usually they are a vehicle for an aspirant to public office who cannot win the nomination of a regular party.

In this instance, the purpose of the Independence Party is to get votes for Kramer which the Democratic mayor might not receive if he ran only as the nominee of the Democrats and the Liberal Party.

Establishment of the party was in accord with a belief held by oldtime politicians that there are hardshell members of both major parties who under no circumstances will vote for the opposing major party. In the present circumstances, it is thought, there are many Republicans in Binghamton who regard Mayor Kramer as head and shoulders above his Republican opponent, Edwin A. Hall. Despite this claimed recognition of the mayor's superiority, it is felt, these same Republicans would refuse to vote for him as a Democrat.

In some mystical way, according to this thinking, the situation is changed if these Republicans have an opportunity to vote for the Independence Party's nominee. It is a mighty fine distinction, but voters of this type are said to be able to forget the fact that the nominee of the Independence Party and the nominee of the Democratic Party is one and the same man.

No one will ever know with scientific precision how many more votes Kramer will get because of the Independence Party than he would have received if this party had not been established. Without any independent nomination, Kramer unquestionably received thousands of Republican votes in 1949. Just why he wouldn't get the support of the same voters this year is an unanswered question.

1) As it turned out Mayor Kramer was re-elected, with the votes of the Independence Party not actually being required.

Did the "professionals" show a knowledge of language in setting up the new party?

(g) *"U.S.-Reich Past Studied Objectively,"* Associated Press, *September 2, 1955.*

Brunswick, Germany. Many Americans and Germans alike failed to see the danger of Hitler's rise . . . Americans had an economic interest in allied victory before they entered World War I . . . The U.S. Senate's rejection of the Versailles Peace Treaty proved President Wilson's ineptness as a political manipulator.

These are "objective" views agreed upon by German and American historians in a week-long conference here. They recommended this week that these views be included in both countries' textbooks to give students a "clear" picture of history. . . .

Prof. Georg Eckert, director of the institute, said it was "extremely fruitful."

"Many historical events which have been presented one-sidedly and with a moralizing tendency in the past now have been neutralized because their causes have been newly identified," he explained.

Eckert said many American textbooks had been revised to conform to the recommendations issued by the last conference in August, 1952. He did not say whether German books were also revised. . . .

1) Do you consider the A.P. story entirely neutral? Consider particularly the selection of examples, the words put in quotation marks, the force of the last sentence from the excerpt.
2) In what way is the problem of the historians complicated by the difficulty in securing "neutral" meanings?
3) Is their problem merely semantic?

---

2 (*a*) *Discuss the level of metaphoric meaning now present or once present in the following common words. Consult your dictionary unless you are sure of the history of the word.*

bar	fret	rod	sun
bent	godlike	rose	supercilious
companion	homely	saintly	sword
depend	homelike	spider	table
egregious	pen	spoon	vein

(b) *From conversations and from themes collect a list of ordinary words which illustrate the prevalence of metaphoric meaning in language.*

---

3. *Which of the following seem concerned primarily with meaning as information, and which with meaning as attitude? Discuss the appropriateness of the word usage in each passage. Indicate such phonetic and syntactic manipulation as appears and try to determine if it seems suitable to the passage. Note that several of the passages will fall somewhere between the extremes of information and attitude, so that it will be necessary to try to get at the writer's purpose. Each passage is by a well-established writer, but the names are not listed until the end of the exercise.*

(a) "It is true, that which I have revealed to you; there is no God, no universe, no human race, no earthly life, no heaven, no hell. It is all a dream—a grotesque and foolish dream. Nothing exists but you. And you are but a thought—a vagrant thought, a homeless thought, wandering forlorn among the empty eternities."

(b) We boast our light; but if we look not wisely on the sun itself, it smites us into darkness. Who can discern those planets that are oft combust, and those stars of brightest magnitude that rise and set with the sun, until the opposite motion of their orbs bring them to such a place in the firmament where they may be seen evening or morning? The light which we have gained was given us, not to be ever staring on, but by it to discover onward things more remote from our knowledge.

(c) The way in which the persecution of Galileo has been remembered is a tribute to the quiet commencement of the most intimate change in outlook which the human race had yet encountered. Since a babe was born in a manger, it may be doubted whether so great a thing has happened with so little stir.

(d) The waking have one and the same world, the sleeping turn aside each into a world of his own.

(e) "For my part, Sir, I think all Christians, whether Papists or Protestants, agree in the essential articles, and that their differences are trivial, and rather political than religious."

(f) No man is an island, entire of itself; every man is a piece of the continent, a part of the main; if a clod be washed away by the sea, Europe is the less, as well as if a promontory were, as well as if a manor of thy friend's or of thine own were; any man's death diminishes me, because I am involved in mankind; and therefore never send to know for whom the bell tolls; it tolls for thee.

(g) In mathematics it is notorious that we start from absurdities to reach a realm of law, and our whole conception of the nature of the world is based on a foundation which we believe to have no existence.

(h) The very first lesson that we have a right to demand that logic shall teach us, is how to make our ideas clear; and a most important one it is, depreciated only by minds who stand in need of it. To know what we think, to be masters of our meaning, will make a solid foundation for great and weighty thought.

(i) Say what you have to say, what you have a will to say, in the simplest, the most direct and exact manner possible, with no surplusage:—there, is the justification of the sentence so fortunately born, "entire, smooth, and round," that it needs no punctuation and also (that is the point!) of the most elaborate period, if it be right in its elaboration.

(j) The truth of an idea is not a stagnant property inherent in it. Truth happens to an idea. It becomes true, is made true by events. Its verity is in fact an event, a process, the process namely of its verifying itself, its verification. Its validity is the process of its validation.

(k) Pyramids, arches, obelisks, were but the irregularities of vain-glory, and wild enormities of ancient magnanimity. But the most magnanimous resolution rests in Christian religion, which trampleth upon pride, and sits on the neck of ambition, humbly pursuing that infallible perpetuity, unto which all others must diminish their diameters, and be properly seen in the angles of contingency.

(1) I have drawn up my chair to my two tables. Two tables! . . . One of them has been familiar to me from earliest years. It is a commonplace object of that environment which I call the world . . . Table No. 2 is my scientific table. It is a more recent acquaintance and I do not feel so familiar with it . . . It is mostly emptiness. Sparsely scattered in that emptiness are numerous electrical charges rushing about with great speed; but their combined bulk amounts to less than a billionth of the bulk of the table itself.

(m) When we run over libraries, persuaded of these principles, what havoc must we make? If we take in our hand any volume; of divinity or school metaphysics, for instance; let us ask, *Does it contain any abstract reasoning concerning quantity or number?* No. *Does it contain any experimental reasoning concerning matter of fact and existence?* No. Commit it then to the flames: for it can contain nothing but sophistry and illusion.

(n) If I like tomatoes and you do not, it is idle to discuss whether that is because we both experience the same physical tastes but value them differently, or because we have a common standard of valuation but experience different physical tastes. The alternatives are only verbally different, because there is no conceivable means of deciding between them.

(o) Look sharply after your thoughts. They come unlooked for, like a new bird seen on your trees, and, if you turn to your usual task, disappear; and you shall never find the perception again; never, I say—but perhaps years, ages, and I know not what events and worlds may lie between you and its return.

(p) As from the union of two opposite germ-cells begins a life, so from the contact of northern and southern air had sprung something which before had not been. As a new life, a focus of activity, begins to develop after its kind and grows by what it feeds on, so in the air that complex of forces began to develop and grow strong. A new storm had been born.

(q) The one common note of all this country is the haunting presence of the ocean. A great faint sound of breakers follows you high up into the inland canyons; the roar of water dwells in the clean, empty rooms of Monterey as in a shell upon the chimney; go where you will you have but to pause and listen to hear the voice of the Pacific.

(r) This, then, is the end of your universal education and civilization, and contempt of the ignorance of the Middle Ages and of their chivalry. Not only do you declare yourselves too indolent to labor for daughters and wives, and too poor to support them, but you have made the neglected and distracted creatures hold it for an honor to be independent of you, and shriek for some hold on the mattock for themselves. Believe it or not, as you may, there has not been so low a level of thought reached by any race, since they grew to be male and female out of starfish, or chickweed, or whatever else they have been made from, by natural selection,—according to modern science.

(s) We shall go on to the end, we shall fight in France, we shall fight on the seas and oceans, we shall fight with growing confidence and growing strength in the air, we shall defend our Island, whatever the cost may be, we shall fight on the beaches, we shall fight on the landing grounds, we shall fight in the fields and in the streets, we shall fight in the hills; we shall never surrender. . . .

(t) And at last, in its curved and imperceptible fall, the sun sank low, and from its glowing white changed to a dull red without rays and without heat, as if about to go out suddenly, stricken to death by the touch of that gloom brooding over a crowd of men.

(u) In fact, precisely at this transitional point of its nightly roll into darkness the great and particular glory of the Egdon waste began, and nobody could be said to understand the heath who had not been there at such a time. It could best be felt when it could not be clearly seen, its complete effect and explanation lying in this and the succeeding hours before the next dawn: then, and only then, did it tell its true tale. The spot was, indeed, a near relation of night, and when night showed itself an apparent tendency to gravitate together could be perceived in its shades and the scene. The sombre stretch of rounds and hollows seemed to rise and meet the evening gloom in pure sympathy, the heath exhaling darkness as rapidly as the heavens precipitated it. And so the obscurity in the air and the obscurity in the land closed together in a black fraternization towards which each advanced half-way.

The passages were written by the following:

(a) Samuel Clemens
(*the devil is imagined speaking*)
(b) John Milton
(c) A. N. Whitehead
(d) Heraclitus
(e) James Boswell
(*Sam Johnson is the speaker*)
(f) John Donne
(g) Havelock Ellis
(h) C. S. Pierce
(i) Walter Pater
(j) William James
(k) Thomas Browne
(l) A. S. Eddington
(m) David Hume
(n) Herbert Dingle
(o) Ralph Waldo Emerson
(p) George R. Stewart
(q) Robert Louis Stevenson
(r) John Ruskin
(s) Winston Churchill
(t) Joseph Conrad
(u) Thomas Hardy

4. Discuss the history of the following words, paying particular attention to how they became part of the Modern English vocabulary: whether by (1) composition and derivation, (2) borrowing, (3) change in meaning, (4) new creation. Try to show how these words illustrate points about language history made in the last section of this chapter.

(a) architect   disposition   professional
akin   exile   solicitude
amphiboly   extremist   spinsterhood
beleaguer   falsify   symbolic
benefit   monarchical   wayward
companion   obliquely   wisdom
contraband   parable   witchcraft
decisive   parachute   withstand

(b) call   frail   silk
describe   fragile   sister
deliberately   gift   sloop
dream   plow   tulip
egg   reason   weak
eventful   sever   window

(c) { truth / veracity }   { people / folk }   { rear / raise }

{ fat / corpulent }   { guardian / warden }   { shoot / skoot }

{ help / assistance }   { regal / royal }   { shirt / skirt }

(d) discard   bayonet   boycott
engine   boy   chimera
idiot   conceit   dunce
propaganda   crafty   gas
quick   facile   mentor
scissors   fame   milliner
starve   impertinent   panic
stool   knight   quisling
wade   philippic   silhouette
wretch   seduce   tantalize

---

5. Write a complete history of one of the following words, referring to the Oxford English Dictionary. Show how changes in the meaning of the word reflect social change.

enthusiasm	nature	income
genius	landlord	law
criticise	tenant	order
dogmatic	tax	progress
constitution (law)	usury	ego

---

6. *The following consists of parallel passages from Matthew 8: 1–4. By careful study and comparison, using your dictionary, you can learn a great deal about the development of English. Study the passages systematically. For example, the first verse gives examples 1) of the sound law about long vowel changes, 2) of the change in syntax from an inflectional system to one relying chiefly on word order and function words, and 3) of changes in words (cf.,* menigu: cumpanyes: multitudes: crowds).

A = *Old English* (Ca. 1000 A.D.)
B = *Wycliffe Version* (Ca. 1400)
C = *King James Version* (17th Century)
D = *Revised Standard* (20th Century)

(1) A: Soþlice þa se Haelend of þaem munte nyþer astah, þa fyligdon him micele menigu.

 B: Forsothe when Jhesus hadde comen doun fro the hil, many cumpanyes folewiden hym.

 C: When he was come down from the mountain, great multitudes followed him.

 D: When he came down from the mountain, great crowds followed him . . .

(2) A: þa genealaehte an hreofla to him, and hine to him geeaþmedde, and þus cwaeþ: Dryhten, gif þu wilt, þu miht me geclaensian.

 B: And loo! a leprouse man cummynge worshipide hym, sayinge, I wole; be thou maad clene. And anoon the lepre of hym was clensid.

 C: And behold, there came a leper and worshipped him, saying, Lord, if thou wilt, thou canst make me clean.

D: . . . and behold, a leper came to him and knelt before him, saying, "Lord, if you will, you can make me clean."

(3) A: þa astrehte se Haelend his hand, and hrepode hine, and þus cwaeþ: Ic wille; beo geclaensod. And his hreofla waes hraedlice geclaensod.

B: And Jhesus, holdynge forthe the hond touchide hym, sayinge, I wole; be thou maad clene. And anoon the lepre of hym was clensid.

C: And Jesus put forth his hand and touched him, saying, I will; be thou clean. And immediately his leprosy was cleansed.

D: And he stretched out his hand and touched him, saying, "I will: be clean." And immediately his leprosy was cleansed.

(4) A: þa cwaeþ se Haelend to him: Warna þe þaet þu hit naenegum men ne secge; ac gang, aetiewe þe paem sacerde, and bring heom þa laec þe Moyses bebead on heora gecyþnesse.

B: And Jhesus saith to hym, See, say thou to no man; but go, shewe thee to prestis, and offre that ʒifte that Moyses comaundide, into witnessing to hem.

C: And Jesus saith unto him, See thou tell no man; but go thy way, shew thyself to the priests, and offer the gift that Moses commanded, for a testimony unto them.

D: And Jesus said to him, "See that you say nothing to anyone; but go show yourself to the priest, and offer the gift that Moses commanded, for a proof to the people."

RECOMMENDED READINGS: LANGUAGE

Leonard Bloomfield, *Language*. New York: Henry Holt & Co., 1933.

John B. Carroll, *The Study of Language*. Cambridge: Harvard University Press, 1953.

Ferdinand de Saussure, *Cours de linguistique général*. Paris: Payot, 1931.

William Entwistle, *Aspects of Language*. London: Faber and Faber, 1953.

Charles Fries, *The Structure of English*. New York: Harcourt, Brace & Co., 1952.

J. B. Greenough and G. L. Kittredge, *Words and Their Ways in English Speech*. New York: The Macmillan Co., 1920.

R. M. S. Heffner, *General Phonetics*. Madison: University of Wisconsin Press, 1950.

Daniel Jones, *The Phoneme: Its Nature and Use*. Cambridge, England: W. Heffer, 1950.

Charlton G. Laird, *The Miracle of Language*. Cleveland: The World Publishing Company, 1953.

H. L. Mencken, *The American Language*. New York: Alfred A. Knopf, 1949.

Fernand Mossé, *Esquisse d'une histoire de la langue Anglaise*. Lyon: IAC, 1947.

H. Pedersen, translated by J. W. Spargo, *Linguistic Science in the Nineteenth Century*. Cambridge: Harvard University Press, 1931.

Simeon Potter, *Our Language*. Baltimore: Penguin Books, 1954.

Edward Sapir, *Language*. New York: Harcourt, Brace Co., 1921.

L. P. Smith, *The English Language*. New York: Henry Holt & Co., 1912.

E. H. Sturtevant, *An Introduction to the Linguistic Science*. New Haven: Yale University Press, 1947.

VALIDITY: DEDUCTIVE LOGIC

LANGUAGE is an essential tool in communication of thought, but confusions and difficulties occur when this tool does not operate efficiently or when it is employed improperly. We have sought to analyze the nature of language and to clarify some of the relationships that exist between the word and its meanings in order to eradicate obstacles to the proper operation of thinking. We must now turn to an analysis of what proper thinking is.

Thought involves a search for principles which will solve problems. This search for principles, which is a primary aspect of thinking, proceeds properly when *logic* is used, that is, when certain rules are followed. Just as the game of chess is played according to certain rules of procedure, so also thinking requires the application of certain rules if thought is to be successful.

There are two kinds of logic that can be distinguished. On the one hand there is *deductive logic*, which pertains to the elements of necessity in all proper thinking. On the other hand there is *inductive logic*, which pertains to the elements of *probability* and *reliability* in all proper thinking. In this chapter we shall investigate deductive logic.

Deductive logic involves the drawing out of those implicit beliefs which we are obligated to accept if we accept certain other beliefs. Very often we are not aware of the obligations incurred by our acceptance of certain views, as in the following short dialogue:

Mr. Jones: I believe that anyone who is for socialized medicine is a communist sympathizer.

Mr. Smith: Of course you know that your boss is for socialized medicine.

Mr. Jones: Oh.

Mr. Jones suddenly became aware of how the acceptance of one set of beliefs often requires the acceptance of other perhaps less-desirable beliefs. Deductive logic, therefore, shows us what *necessarily* follows from the endorsement of a given set of ideas.

The workings of deductive logic can be shown by examining a "live" situation in which deductive logic plays an important role. Assume that a student has been assigned to write an essay on a controversial subject—the value of the United Nations. Put simply, the problem of a person writing such an essay is *to come to a conclusion* about the United Nations. Of course he may well simply parrot the views of his family and friends, ignoring anything that contradicts a conclusion which he has accepted ready-made. There is, in fact, little doubt that many persons adopt just such a procedure, simply reiterating beliefs that have been handed down to them.

However, let us assume that our writer, regardless of how prejudiced he may really be, prides himself on being completely unprejudiced. He is aware that he must reject "hearsay" and that his opinions must be based on fact and documentation. Thus he will look up articles in newspapers and periodicals, and, if he is interested, he will get other viewpoints in conversations and conferences. He may even go on a field trip to the United Nations headquarters—"to see for himself." When the time comes for him to write his essay he will have before him a collection of notes containing various kinds of information and varying shades of opinion. His problem now is *to draw a conclusion from the varied data in his notes*.

Since he knows that a good theme is made up of an introduction, body, and conclusion, he feels certain that by proceeding from introduction to conclusion, with the help of the data he has accumulated, he should be able to write a successful essay. His first problem is clearly defined: how shall he begin? The simplest method will be to explain what he intends to prove, which will necessitate a study of his notes. These notes show, first, that while at the United Nations he heard, in translation, a bitter attack on the United States delivered by the Soviet Ambassador, who called us "warmongers" and "victims of a bloodthirsty Wall Street." Second, his notes refer to his meeting with an English-speaking employee of the United Nations who advanced what seemed to our writer cynical observations about "McCarthyism" in the United States. Third, his notes contain several critical quotations selected from a number of articles. Quite unaware how much he has been guided by prejudice, he believes that his notes suggest no neglect either of fact or of scholarship.

With this array of material the student is ready for the introduction to his essay. He begins: "In this essay I shall try to demonstrate, through facts and figures, that the United Nations is dominated by the Communists and their propaganda. I will not ask you to believe me, but I will ask that you believe the results of firsthand, on-the-spot investigations. I will ask you to believe what many prominent men have said about the United Nations. The United Nations is a waste of time and money; it is even worse than that, it is a serious threat to our beloved country."

The introduction out of the way, the student now turns to the body of the paper. This part is comparatively simple, for he does not quite have to "spread" himself as he did in the introduction. He need merely set down the information he has gathered together, all of which tends to prove his point. Perhaps with an eye to his instructor, he will try to maintain the high style of his introduction: a few polysyllables and a few complex and complicated sentences will help with the over-all effect. Then, having completed the body of his theme, the student adds his conclusion: "The United Nations is a waste of time and money, and a threat to our nation."

With considerable confidence he hands in his essay. But

several days later, when the paper is returned, he finds he has
not received the high grade that he confidently expected in
view of the amount of "research" he had done and in view of
the attention he had paid to "good" writing. In fact, the
instructor had written some critical comments. The theme is
"wordy . . . the conclusion does not *logically follow*, and the
evidence is not *reliable*."

At this point the student finds himself in a real dilemma.
What's wrong? As far as reliable evidence is concerned—what
can be better than actually going to the United Nations and
seeing for one's self? Hasn't he done this? And, finally, what
does the instructor mean when he says "conclusion does not
logically follow"? The theme had been carefully organized
according to the time-honored principle of introduction, body,
and conclusion. This should have taken care of the "logic" of
the paper. But it didn't. Then what is meant by "logic"? When
does a conclusion follow logically? These are the questions that
often bother people. The answer to them will give us an understanding of deductive logic. But before we begin this task,
several introductory observations must be made.

First, the instructor's criticism of the essay does not mean
that he is necessarily in disagreement with the student's conclusions. Frequently students believe that a low mark on a
theme indicates that the instructor does not approve of the
student's point of view. But it may well be that the instructor
agrees that the United Nations is a waste of time and money.
His note to the student is not a criticism of the conclusion,
but rather it is a criticism of the way in which the student
has arrived at the conclusion. He is saying that such an ending is not legitimately linked to the kind of evidence the
student has submitted; in short, that the introduction, the body,
and the conclusion are not properly connected.

Second, the student has fallen into many of the pitfalls that
were discussed in the first chapter. He has permitted emotions
and personal feelings to permeate his argument. As a result the
instructor has automatically become suspicious. Any paper
that is too emotional in tone can arouse the suspicion that the
writer is attempting to appeal to emotion rather than to

reasonable thinking. As we pointed out in the first chapter, the intensity of emotion behind a belief does not make it true. For thousands of years people have believed in the most irrational superstitions, without making these views any more reliable.

With these general observations we are now ready to examine in detail one half of the instructor's note: "Conclusion does not *logically follow*. . . ." What does it mean to say that something "logically follows"?

ASSOCIATION, DESCRIPTION, AND ARGUMENT

Most people believe that they are logical, but few have any knowledge of what being logical means. When someone wishes to make his argument stronger, he claims that he is "logical" and his opponent is "illogical." Our student may very well claim that he has drawn the "logical conclusion" from the facts, but he probably has only the vaguest idea of what logic actually is.

To begin to understand what being logical means, let us distinguish among three sets of sentences:

1. I'm going to college. The first American college for women opened in 1834. I prefer my classes in the morning.

2. The grass is green. The sun is shining brightly. The clouds are white and fleecy.

3. All men are animals. All animals require food and shelter. Therefore, all men require food and shelter.

All three sets of statements do have some kind of order. The first set is in an *order of association*. A word or phrase in one sentence by association suggests something else, and this, in turn, suggests still something further. In this order our minds merely drift. I think of college; I am reminded that the first American college for women opened in 1834; something peculiar to myself associates this idea with morning classes. The connections between the statements are subjective. Another person might be reminded of something entirely different.

The second group of sentences are in an *order of description*.

The statements describe an existing phenomenon: the weather. This descriptive order is not quite so subjective as the order of association. Whereas the sentences in the associative order are not controlled by any objective reference (i.e., they are controlled only by some psychological motivation), the sentences of the descriptive order are controlled by some objective referent, viz., the weather. Furthermore, the sentences in the descriptive order could be completely reshuffled and the same situation would still be described. One arrangement might be more effective than another, but the description would remain essentially the same. In the descriptive order no claim is asserted that any one of the sentences is true or false because of the other statements. In this respect the descriptive order differs from the third set of sentences, which is the *order of argument*.

The key to the *order of argument* in the third set of statements is the term *therefore*, which implies that the sentence after the *therefore* is in some way derived from the other sentences. *Therefore*, or synonyms like *thus, it follows, from this you can see*, etc., suggest the presence of an argument. The "therefore" can of course be implied without being stated. A connection between the third sentence and the preceding sentences would still be implied, even if "therefore" were omitted. The presence of the "therefore" is merely symptomatic of what is of major importance in logic; that is, that one of the statements is assumed to follow as a consequence of other statements.

VALIDITY

If we accept the first two statements as true in the argument on page 114, viz., "All men are animals" and "All animals require food and shelter," then the last statement, "All men require food and shelter," is *necessarily true*. When an argument has this kind of relationship, when the conclusion has this necessary connection to the premises, the argument is *logical*, or, in the more precise term of logicians, *valid*. Any argument is said to be valid, or logical, if there is one sentence (called the *con-*

clusion) that follows necessarily from the other sentences (called *premises*). The conclusion follows necessarily from the premises when no other statement is possible as a result of the previous statements. Thus if anyone tells us that what he says "logically follows," then he means that his conclusion, or a synonymous statement, *must* follow. If there is even one other alternative possible, then, strictly speaking, his argument is not valid.

It is important to note, however, that the validity of the above argument does *not* depend upon the truth of the premises. An argument can be valid even if the premises and the conclusion are false. For example, the following argument is valid:

> All boys are girls.
> All girls are unicorns.
> Therefore, all boys are unicorns.

Validity, as we shall see, depends upon the arrangement of the elements in each statement, not on truth or falsity. Certain arrangements make an argument logical; others make it illogical. Once an argument has a correct arrangement, that is, is valid, *then and only then* do true premises entail a true conclusion.

Thus when the instructor said that the student's conclusion did not "follow logically" he meant that it was not the only possibility. Even if all the data in the "body"—or the premises—were true the student's conclusion would still not necessarily be connected to those premises.

ARGUMENT AND LANGUAGE

Being logical, therefore, involves a relationship between a group of statements called *premises* (or evidence) and another statement called a *conclusion*. When these statements are properly arranged our arguments are logical; when they are improperly arranged they are illogical. Thus we shall see that simply because of the arrangement of the elements in the

statements, one of the following arguments is logical while
the other is not:

(1)   All people are weaklings.
       All weaklings are fools.   (Logical)
       Therefore, all people are fools.

(2)   All people are weaklings.
       All fools are weaklings.   (Not logical)
       Therefore, all people are fools.

The words in both arguments are the same. But the seemingly innocent change of "All weaklings are fools" to "All fools
are weaklings" makes (2) illogical. The major problem becomes
one of discovering the principles that make certain arrangements logical. Just as in mathematics certain rules are employed
to determine which arithmetical operations are allowable, in
logic rules are employed to determine allowable conclusions.

In analyzing the logic of paragraphs or essays we are concerned only with the specific premises and conclusion. But
these statements are often difficult to extract. Some paragraphs
have to be read and reread before we can be sure of what
specific premises and conclusion are being asserted. Sometimes
the conclusion appears at the beginning or middle of the paragraph, sometimes the premises contain an abundance of facts
and data, but often the difficulty may be traced to the com-
plexity of expression. No one will deny that the writer is
frequently governed by the desire to make his argument more
persuasive through his choice of words and illustrations. Nor
will anyone deny that a barren, completely abstract argument
is less interesting than one which is enlivened by examples and
emotion-arousing words. But at the same time it is important
to recognize that the average writer—whether of fiction or non-
fiction—is generally more concerned with facts and words than
with logic. As a result his arguments are frequently hidden by
excess verbiage, irrelevancies, and loose organization. Therefore,
whenever the ideas expressed by a piece of writing are to be
examined critically, the basic argument must be disentangled
from the surplus language that obscures it. We must shear away

all that is not directly concerned with premises and conclusion. To analyze the logic of a paragraph all phrases that are "padding" must be discounted.

Let us assume that the major argument of our student's United Nations essay could be condensed in the following way:

> After listening to Malik and other foreigners at the United Nations I felt that the United Nations is generally very critical of United States policy. My reading has pretty well shown that a major characteristic of those following the Communist line is harsh criticism of United States policy. I must conclude that the United Nations follows— even if it doesn't always know it—the Communist line.

What is the argument presented in this paragraph?

Generally, it is easier to begin by finding the conclusion. The premises are usually more difficult to discover. In this instance the conclusion seems to be fairly obvious. Shorn of words and statements unessential to the basic argument, such as "even if it doesn't always know it," the conclusion is, "The United Nations follows the Communist line." This is the point the student really wishes to make. Now we must find the premises that support this conclusion. In other words, we must look for the evidence which the student has presented. With the extraneous words omitted, two premises are given as evidence:

(1) The United Nations is very critical of the United States.
(2) Those following the Communist line are very critical of the United States.

These are the two major reasons the student gives. All the other words are either meant to reinforce these two statements or else they are emotive words utilized for emphasis or padding.

Thus the basic argument in the above paragraph reduces to:

Premises (1) The United Nations is very critical of the United States.
(2) The Communists are very critical of the United States.

Conclusion (3) Therefore, the United Nations follows the
Communist line.

When the basic premises and conclusion have been extracted
and shorn of all excess verbiage, the first step in checking the
logic of the argument has been accomplished.

EXERCISES

*Which of the following are arguments? Give the premises
and conclusion in each argument.*

(1) All men are wealthy, all men are healthy, and all men
are stealthy.

(2) We have met the enemy and they are ours.

(3) "A boy's will is the wind's will, and the thoughts of
youth are long, long thoughts." (Longfellow, "My Lost
Youth".)

(4) "A novel has for its aim, even for external aim, the
description of a whole human life or of many human lives, and
therefore its writer should have a clear and firm conception
of what is good and bad in life. . . ." (Tolstoy, "Introduction
to the Works of Guy De Maupassant.")

(5) "And of all the things against which a prince must
guard himself the first is being an object of contempt and
hatred. Liberality leads you to both of these. Hence there is
more wisdom in keeping a name for stinginess, which produces
a bad reputation without hatred than in striving for the name
of liberal, only to be forced to get the name of rapacious, which
brings forth both bad reputation and hatred." (Machiavelli,
The Prince, Ch. 16.)

(6) The historian's patriotism is simply love of the truth.
He is not a man of any particular race or of any particular
country. He is a citizen of all countries and he speaks in the
name of all civilization. (Lanfrey's *History of Napoleon*, Vol. 3,
p. 2 [1870].)

(7) When I *hear* music I fear no danger, I am invulnerable,
I see no foe. I am related to the earliest times, and to the
latest. (Thoreau, *Journals*, Jan. 13, 1857.)

(8) *Macbeth.* If it were done when 'tis done, then 'twere well
It were done quickly: if the assassination
Could trammel up the consequence, and catch
With his surcease, success; that but this blow
Might be the be-all and the end-all here,
But here, upon this bank and shoal of time,
We'd jump the life to come. . . .

(Shakespeare, *Macbeth*, Act I, Scene VII.)

(9) As I walked along in the sun I remembered old Cotter's
words and tried to remember what had happened afterwards
in the dream. I remembered that I had noticed long velvet
curtains and a swinging lamp of antique fashion. I felt that I
had been very far away, in some land where the customs were
strange—in Persia, I thought . . . But I could not remember
the end of the dream. (Joyce, *Dubliners*, "The Sisters.")

(10) There is today everywhere in Europe a sickly irrita-
bility and sensitivity to pain, a repulsive, unrestrained com-
plaining—a softening which with the help of religion and
philosophical nonsense seeks to disguise itself as something
superior. There is a regular cult of suffering. The unmanliness
of what is called "sympathy" in such circles of visionaries is
the first thing that strikes my eye. (Nietzsche, *Beyond Good
and Evil.*)

TYPES OF LOGICAL STATEMENTS

In extracting the premises and conclusion of the student's
argument on the United Nations only the first step in logical
analysis has been performed. The argument has been reduced
to three statements, but no means have been established to
test whether the conclusion must of necessity follow from the
premises, that is, whether the argument is valid. Let us again
state the two premises and conclusion:

(1) The United Nations is very critical of the United States.
(2) The Communists are very critical of the United States.
(3) Therefore, the United Nations follows the Communist
line.

These statements have two characteristics in common: (a) they are made up of subjects and predicates; (b) unlike other possible sentences that might refer to some part of the United Nations or to some Communists, these sentences refer to the *entire* United Nations or to *all* the Communists. It is true that no specific reference is made to the *entire* United Nations or to *all* the Communists. But, unless the student himself states that he only meant *some* of the United Nations or *some* of the Communists, we are probably correct in assuming that the sentences refer to *all*. Whenever an argument's validity is being tested, it is important to know whether the premises and conclusion refer to *all*, or to *some*, or to *none*. For this reason the United Nations argument should undergo the following transformation:

(1) All (the entire) United Nations is very critical of the United States.

(2) All the Communists are very critical of the United States.

(3) Therefore, all (the entire) United Nations follows the Communist line.

Very often it is unclear whether a writer or a speaker is referring to *all* or *some* or *none* of a given group. When a person says "men are basically good" he very obviously does not mean "No men are basically good," but he might mean "*All* men are basically good" or "*Some* men are basically good." But when we seek to check the logic of an argument we must ask the speaker if he means "all" or "some." For purposes of logical analysis, sentences are always transformed so that they begin either with an *all*, or a *some*, or with a *no*. Thus four possible types of *logical statements* can be distinguished:

(1) All (subject) is/are (predicate);
    i.e., All men are mortal.
(2) No (subject) is/are (predicate);
    i.e., No man is immortal.
(3) Some (subject) is/are (predicate);
    i.e., Some men are long-lived.

(4) Some (subject) is/are not (predicate);
   i.e., Some men are not long-lived.

We shall call (1) a *universal-affirmative,* (2) a *universal-negative,* (3) a *particular-affirmative,* and (4) a *particular-negative.* To check the logic of an argument each sentence in the argument must be reduced to one of these four types. Even where such transformation seems awkward, this rule must be followed. Thus, a sentence such as "Socrates is mortal" should be changed to read "All of Socrates is mortal" in spite of its awkwardness. No matter how complicated the statement it must be changed into one of the four types listed. Logicians often use other types, but most sentences can be transformed into one of the four types, and, as we shall see, they afford us a means of testing the validity of most arguments.

Since it is rather clumsy to refer to the *universal-affirmative* as "All (subject) is (predicate)" and to the *universal-negative* as "No (subject) is (predicate)," let us simplify by substituting "X" for "subject" and "Y" for "predicate." Our four types of logical statement will now read:

Universal-affirmative	— All X is Y.
Universal-negative	— No X is Y.
Particular-affirmative	— Some X is Y.
Particular-negative	— Some X is not Y.

These four logical forms are the only ones needed for logical analysis. No matter what "X" and "Y" may refer to, if a sentence can be reduced to one of the above types, it is ready for logical analysis. The United Nations argument may now undergo the following final change:

(1) All the United Nations is very critical of the United States *becomes* All X is Y.

(2) All who follow the Communist line are very critical of the United States *becomes* All Z is Y.

(3) Therefore, all the United Nations follows the Communist line *becomes* Therefore, All X is Z.

Note two points:

(1) Each letter replaces a given subject or predicate. When a new subject or predicate is introduced a new letter must be used. For this reason a new letter "Z" is used to replace the third expression, "Those who follow the Communist line."

(2) "X," "Y," and "Z" are arbitrary symbols: a, b, c; or 1, 2, 3; or any set of marks can be used to designate the given subjects or predicates.

Once we have changed our argument into the form which contains "X," "Y," and "Z," and *some, all,* or *no,* we need not worry about the original argument. We may work solely with these symbols. If the arrangement of these symbols abides by certain rules, the argument is legitimate, that is, *valid;* otherwise it is not legitimate, that is, it is *invalid.*

Transform each of the following statements into one of the four types of logical statement.

Example: Children are precocious = All children are precocious = All X is Y.

(1) Reliable testimony is certainly important.

(2) Every large city has its slums full of sickness and criminality.

(3) The two-party system ought to be defended by every democratic American.

(4) There can be no prosperity in America as long as poverty prevails in Europe.

(5) Her eyes are green.

(6) John's hair is red.

(7) Without exception great statesmen have not been lacking in vision.

(8) You can fool some of the people some of the time.

(9) Frailty, thy name is woman.

(10) Social justice does not survive in a vacuum.

(11) The learned reader must have observed that in the course of this mighty work I have often translated passages out

of the best ancient authors without quoting the original, or without taking the least notice of the book from whence they were borrowed. (Fielding, *Tom Jones*, Bk. XII.)

(12) Most of the crimes which disturb the internal peace of society are produced by the restraints which the necessary, but unequal, laws of property have imposed on the appetites of mankind, by confining to a few the possession of those objects that are coveted by many. (Gibbon, *History of the Decline and Fall of the Roman Empire*, Vol. I, Ch. 4.)

THE RULES OF DISTRIBUTION

Once an argument has been transformed into symbolic form an important part of logical analysis has been accomplished. The next step involves the application of the Rules of Distribution.

Perhaps the best way to understand these rules is to examine their operation in one of the logical types, e.g., "All X is Y." In the form "All X is Y" reference is made to *all of* X, but *not to all of* Y. Thus the statement "All humans are mammals" says something about *all humans*, but *not* about *all mammals*. The statement does not imply that *all* mammals are *humans*; actually many mammals are not humans, for example, monkeys. Whenever the *entire* X or Y is involved, then the terms X or Y are called *distributed* terms. Whenever the whole of X or Y is *not* involved, the terms are said to be *undistributed*. From this analysis it follows that in the *universal-affirmative* "All X is Y," the subject X is *distributed*, but Y is *undistributed*.

The *universal-negative*, "No X is Y," may seem to involve difficulties, but its distribution is actually easy to determine. First of all, the statement "None of X is Y" really means that the entire X is completely removed from the entire Y. Thus "No humans are monkeys" means that the entire human race is excluded from the entire race of monkeys and the entire race of monkeys is excluded from the entire race of humans. Since the *universal-negative* statement is concerned with the entire

X and the entire Y, *both* X *and* Y are considered to be *distributed*.

The distribution of the *particular-affirmative* is also not very difficult to discern. The *particular-affirmative* says "Some X is Y." It should be obvious that in both "X" and "Y" there is no mention of all of "X" or "Y." In "Some students are hard workers," reference is not made to *all* students, nor does the statement say that *all* hard workers are students. Since there is no reference to an entire group in the *particular-affirmative*, the "X" and "Y" are *both undistributed*.

The distribution of the *particular-negative*, "Some X is not Y," is a little more difficult to determine. Since reference is to "Some X" it is easy to see that "X" is *undistributed*. But how about "Y"? At first glance "Y" seems to be undistributed, since it does not refer to entirety of any kind. But consider the statement "Some colleges are not coeducational." Doesn't it say that some colleges are excluded from the entirety of that group called coeducational? In short, something *is* said about the entire group of coeducational colleges, viz., that some colleges are excluded from the entire group of coeducational colleges. Thus in a *particular-negative* the "X" is undistributed, but the "Y" is distributed.

The following diagram of the *distribution rules* might prove helpful.

	X	Y
All X is Y	Distributed	Undistributed
No X is Y	Distributed	Distributed
Some X is Y	Undistributed	Undistributed
Some X is not Y	Undistributed	Distributed

SYLLOGISM

With our knowledge of (1) arguments, (2) types of logical statements, and (3) rules of distribution, we are now able to check the validity of most arguments. The simplest form of ar-

gument is one consisting of two premises and a conclusion, such
as in the following:

> All men are mortal.   *middle term*
> All college professors are men.
> Therefore all college professors are mortal.

An argument of this kind is called a *syllogism*. What the
syllogism seeks to do is to make explicit in the conclusion the
connection that is implicit in the premises. Thus in "All college professors are mortal" the two terms *college professors* and
mortal are connected in the conclusion even though they are
not explicitly connected in the premises. The justification for
making such a connection is based on the fact that the term
men links together *college professors* and *mortal*. This link is
called the *middle term. Every syllogism must contain one term
which is shared by both premises and does not appear in the
conclusion.* which is the "men"

Perhaps the nature of the connection in the syllogism can
be shown by use of the following symbolic device. Let us
consider *men, mortal,* and *college professors* as referring to circles. "All men are mortals" would then be symbolized by placing the circle   men   in the circle   mortal.   Thus we obtain
the following:

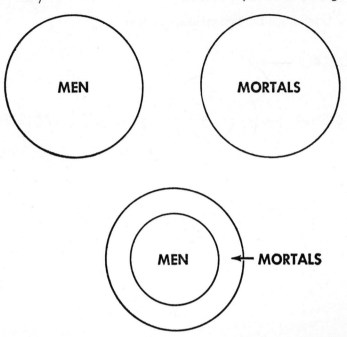

By applying the same procedure to the second premise, "All college professors are men," we obtain the following:

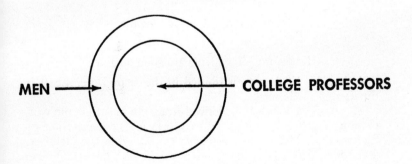

Combining the two premises we get:

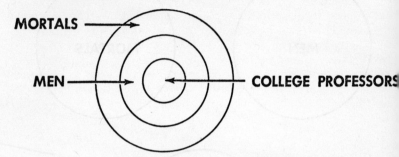

It should be apparent that the circle of *college professors* is included in the circle of *mortals,* that is, that "All college professors are mortals." By drawing the two premises we have implicitly drawn the conclusion. We have "connected" *college professors* to *mortal.*

The discovery of a connection in a syllogism is not always a simple matter and does not always guarantee validity. For this reason the validity of a syllogism can be determined by following four general rules:

(1) *In any syllogism the middle term must be distributed at least once.* This condition is satisfied in the following example:

$$X \qquad\qquad Y$$
All intelligent people are good citizens.
$$Z \qquad\qquad X$$
All students are intelligent people.
$$Z \qquad\qquad Y$$

Therefore, all students are good citizens.

Although "X" is not distributed in the second premise, it is distributed in the first.

The basis of this rule is derived from the fact that the conclusion of any syllogism always consists in the connection of the two terms that are not explicitly connected in the premises. Thus in "All students are good citizens" two terms are connected in the conclusion even though they are not explicitly connected in the premises. What justification is there for making such a connection? The answer is that the third term, the middle term, "intelligent people," links together "students" and "good citizens." If there were no such link then, indeed, there would be no justification for the conclusion. For this reason the syllogism must have a middle term. Furthermore, the middle term cannot be undistributed in both premises, for if both were undistributed no connection would exist between them. Consider the following syllogism that does not contain a distributed middle term:

> All men are animals.
> All dogs are animals.
> Therefore, all men are dogs.

We can probably recognize intuitively that this argument is not logical. But the reason is that the word "animals" in the first premise does not necessarily refer to the same creatures as those referred to by the word "animals" in the second premise. There is no real link between the premises and, therefore, the conclusion cannot be legitimately asserted. But suppose that the syllogism did have a distributed middle term:

> All men are animals.
> All animals are ferocious.
> Therefore, all men are ferocious.

In this example "animals" in the second premise is distributed and therefore refers to *all* animals. Since it refers to *all* animals it also includes those designated in the first premise. A genuine link has been established.

(2) A syllogism must also satisfy Rule 2 which states: *Any symbol that is distributed in the conclusion must also be distributed in the premises.* Consider the following syllogism:

>   X   Y
> All men are rational.
>   Z   X
> Socrates is a man.
>   Z   Y
> Therefore, Socrates is rational.

In this syllogism the symbol "Z" is distributed in the conclusion. It is also distributed in the premises. Thus this syllogism satisfies Rule 2.

To understand this rule it is only necessary to refer to the rules of distribution which state that whereas every symbol which refers only to *some* is undistributed, every symbol referring to *all* or the *entirety* is distributed. Clearly, we cannot say that because "some people are bald" that therefore "all people are bald." We cannot say that because "some people are not Communists" that therefore "no people are Communists." A distributed symbol can be undistributed in the conclusion. But an undistributed symbol cannot be distributed in the conclusion. *All* implies *some*, but *some* may or may not imply *all*.

(3) A third rule that must be applied to every syllogism is: *If the two premises are negative then no conclusion necessarily follows.* If no conclusion necessarily follows, the syllogism is not valid. This rule operates in the following instance:

No X is Y	No men are dogs.
No Y is Z	No dogs are rational.
Therefore No X is Z	Therefore No men are rational.

The reason for this rule is implicit in Rule 1. Rule 1 states that the terms must be connected in the premises if they are to be connected in the conclusion. But if the premises deny such connections—and this occurs when both premises are negative—then no conclusion can be drawn. If "men" are not connected to "dogs," and if "dogs" are not connected to "rational," then the premises tell us nothing about whether "men" are or are not connected to "rational." In short, no conclusion can follow from two negative premises.

(4) Finally, a fourth rule states: *If a premise is negative then the conclusion must be negative.* If we were to examine each of the possible combinations of affirmative and negative premises, we would discover that the rule about negative conclusions, like the others, is based on the connection of middle terms. Consider, as one example, the following valid syllogism:

      X   Y

All philosophers are seekers after truth.

      X   Z

Some philosophers are not happy.

            Y   Z

Therefore, some seekers after truth are not happy.

First, "all philosophers" and "some philosophers" are obviously related in that "all philosophers" includes "some philosophers." Second, the second premise states that some philosophers are lacking a characteristic, viz., they are not happy. But since all philosophers are also seekers of truth, therefore some seekers of truth must also be lacking this characteristic. In short, the negative premise entitles us to speak only about what some seekers of truth *are not*. The conclusion must be negative. Similarly, if the second premise had been affirmative, an affirmative conclusion would have been obligatory.

It is important to note that "Some seekers of truth are not happy" is not equivalent to "Some seekers of truth are happy." "Some X is not Y" is not the same as "Some X is Y." Some seekers of truth might very well be unhappy. But the rest might be neither happy nor unhappy. They might be tranquil, apathetic, or indifferent.

Thus every syllogism must satisfy four rules if it is to be considered a valid syllogism:

(1) *The middle term must be distributed at least once.*

(2) *A term that is distributed in the conclusion must be distributed in the premises.*

(3) *Only one premise may be negative.*

(4) *When one premise is negative, the conclusion must be negative.*

If a syllogism violates any one of these rules, it is invalid.

THE VALIDITY OF OUR UNITED NATIONS ARGUMENT

We are finally prepared to find out whether the United Nations argument is or is not valid.

All the United Nations is very critical of the United States.
All those who follow the Communist line are very critical of the United States.
Therefore all the United Nations follows the Communist line.

Transferred to symbols:

> All X is Y
> All Z is Y
> Therefore all X is Z.

It is easy to see that this syllogism is invalid. Since "Y" is undistributed in both premises the syllogism violates Rule 1. At least one of the middle terms must be distributed. What the instructor meant when he said the argument was "illogical" can now be better understood. The premises, the evidence, may have been correct, but the conclusion did not follow from the premises. Both the United Nations and the Communists might be critical of the United States, but this would not necessitate the single conclusion that the United Nations is following the Communist line.[1]

EXERCISES

Each of the following has the form of a syllogism. Test the validity of those which satisfy the basic requirements of the syllogism, and indicate which do not satisfy the requirements.

(1) No mammals are men.
  All men are mortal.
  Therefore no mammals are mortal.

---

[1] For another method of validating syllogisms see Appendix to this chapter.

(2)   All mules are lazy.
      Some small animals are lazy.   *Inv.*
      Therefore all mules are small animals.

(3)   No professor is illogical.
      No doctor is illogical.   *Inv.*
      Therefore no professor is a doctor.

(4)   All bachelors are eccentric.
      All eccentrics should get married.   *V*
      Therefore all bachelors should get married.

(5)   Some girls are pretty.
      Anne is a girl.   *V*
      Therefore Anne is pretty.

(6)   All dogs have fleas.
      My dog has fleas.   *Inv.*
      Therefore my dog is a dog.

(7)   Some college students are superstitious.
      All superstitious people are ignorant.   *Valid*
      Therefore some college students are ignorant.

(8)   All prizefighters are pugnacious.
      Some prizefighters are not winners.   *Valid*
      Therefore some pugnacious people are not winners.

(9)   No red-blooded Americans like art.
      All who like art are aesthetes.   *V*
      Therefore no red-blooded American is an aesthete.

(10) All men are rational.
      Joe is rational.   *Invalid*
      Therefore Joe is a man.

TRANSLATION OF SENTENCES INTO LOGICAL FORM

The procedures for testing the syllogism can be applied to the
most complicated kinds of reasoning. But arguments are rarely
presented in such a way that their logical form is immediately

apparent. The translation of the statements in the United Nations argument caused no real difficulty. But what, for example, is the proper translation of the following sentence: "Only loyal organizations are acceptable in this country"? It seems to be equivalent to "All loyal organizations are acceptable in this country." But suppose we said, "Only men wear hats." It is obvious that this is not the equivalent of "All men wear hats." Actually, "Only men wear hats" means "All who wear hats are men." Note carefully what has happened in this translation. The subject and predicate have been reversed. "Only loyal organizations are acceptable in this country" becomes the universal-affirmative "All organizations acceptable in this country are loyal." "Only X is Y" is equivalent to "All Y is X."

Again, a statement such as "No organizations but conspiratorial ones are undemocratic" is equivalent to "Only conspiratorial organizations are undemocratic." Since the "No . . . but" is equivalent to "only" it is also translated as a universal-affirmative, with reversed subject and predicate: "All organizations that are undemocratic are conspiratorial." On the other hand, when a sentence is clearly negative, translation into an affirmative statement is not allowable; for example, "X is never Y" is equivalent to "No X is Y," *not* to "All X is never Y." Thus the statement "Women are never satisfied" is translated into the universal-negative, "No women are satisfied."

How should the statement "Social justice rarely survives in a vacuum" be translated: "No social justice is able to survive in a vacuum," or "Some social justice is not able to survive in a vacuum"? The latter probably most accurately represents the logical translation of the sentence, but the first translation may represent what the writer intended. A similar difficulty is encountered in the sentence "If an object is a metal then it is a conductor of electricity." For our purposes this sentence is best translated "All metals are conductors." But there is always the possibility that another translation is more satisfactory. Unless we can ask the writer, we must decide ourselves which is implied by the language of any given statement.

On the other hand, sentences cannot be arbitrarily rearranged during the process of translation. In the same sentence a dis-

tributed subject may be interchanged with a distributed predicate, that is, "No X is Y" is equivalent to "No Y is X." Similarly, undistributed terms are interchangeable, that is, "Some X
is Y" is equivalent to "Some Y is X." But undistributed terms
cannot be interchanged with distributed terms, that is, "All X
is Y" is *not* equivalent to "All Y is X," nor is "Some X is not
Y" equivalent to "Some Y is not X."

ENTHYMEME

Thus far the arguments considered have had explicit premises and conclusions. But often an argument is only partially
expressed. Thus at first glance the following statement might
very well not be considered a syllogism:

People who trade honestly do not get ahead as quickly as
Mr. Jones does.

Nor does it seem like a syllogism when it is transformed into:

       X   Y
No one who trades honestly is one who gets ahead quickly.
     Z   Y
Mr. Jones is one who gets ahead quickly.

But this does not mean that the argument is not a syllogism.
The conclusion is in fact implicit:
       Z   X
"No one who is Mr. Jones is a person who trades honestly."

On the assumption that such a conclusion follows we are able
to check whether the argument is or is not valid. An *enthymeme*
is any syllogistic argument in which premises or conclusion are
not explicitly expressed.

In the above example the conclusion was concealed. But
sometimes one or even both premises are concealed. For example:

He believes in socialized medicine. He must be a communist.

In this example a premise is concealed, viz., "Anyone who believes in socialized medicine must be a communist." Very often premises are deliberately omitted because making them explicit could destroy the truth value of the argument or show its invalidity.

Kuremkwick is prepared under a doctor's supervision. Get Kuremkwick for sure relief!

At first glance this argument might be accepted, but not when the hidden premise is made explicit: "Anything prepared under a doctor's supervision will give sure relief." The argument is valid. But since only true premises guarantee a true conclusion, the falsity of the implicit premise makes the truth of the conclusion dubious.

Finally, some single statements are actually arguments with two concealed premises. For example, there is a well-known ad showing a well-dressed, distinguished-looking man with a glass of whisky in his hand. On the bottom of the ad are the words, "Drink Old Apple Blossom!" This sentence might conceal the following:

All men of distinction should drink Old Apple Blossom.
You are a man of distinction.
You should drink Old Apple Blossom.

SORITES

The student who tries to apply his knowledge of the syllogism to complicated arguments finds that many such arguments are not reducible to the simple two-premise form that is found in the syllogism. Actually most arguments contain more than merely two premises, but syllogistic rules can be applied to such arguments. A frequently used argument is called the *sorites*. The sorites is a series of syllogisms which have been fused together in such a way that various premises and conclusions are suggested but not actually given. Consider, for example, the following argument:

We know that fanatics are people with closed minds. And people of this sort are always opposed to the advancement of knowledge. Such opposition means that they are against progress. To be against progress is to be an enemy of human welfare. Thus fanatics are enemies of human welfare.

By means of the procedures outlined above it is not difficult to transform this paragraph into a series of logical statements:

All fanatics are people with closed minds.
All people with closed minds are opposed to the advancement of knowledge.
All those who are opposed to the advancement of knowledge are against progress.
All those who are against progress are enemies of human welfare.
Therefore, all fanatics are enemies of human welfare.

In this argument notice that the first two premises imply a conclusion that is not expressed, viz., "All fanatics are opposed to the advancement of knowledge." This unexpressed conclusion is then changed into a premise and combines with the third premise, "All those who are opposed to the advancement of knowledge are against progress." As a result, from these two premises can be deduced an unstated conclusion, "All fanatics are against progress." In turn this conclusion is combined with the fourth premise and the simple syllogistic rules can be used to deduce the stated conclusion, "Therefore, all fanatics are enemies of human welfare." This kind of argument is a sorites. In general two main features characterize the sorites: (1) Only the last conclusion is expressed, and (2) all conclusions, except the last, become unexpressed premises.

To discover whether a sorites is valid, the same rules are employed as those used with the ordinary syllogism. Thus in our example we would first check the validity of the first argument that contains an unexpressed conclusion:

All fanatics are people with closed minds. (First premise.)
All people with closed minds are opposed to the advancement of knowledge. (Second premise.)

Therefore, all fanatics are those who are opposed to the advancement of knowledge. (Unexpressed conclusion.)

We would then proceed to test the validity of the second argument:

All fanatics are those who are opposed to the advancement of knowledge. (Unexpressed premise.)
All those who are opposed to the advancement of knowledge are against progress. (Third premise.)
Therefore, all fanatics are those who are against progress. (Unexpressed conclusion.)

Finally, we would conclude by testing the validity of the third argument:

All fanatics are those who are against progress. (Unexpressed premise.)
All those who are against progress are enemies of human welfare. (Fourth premise.)
Therefore, all fanatics are enemies of human welfare. (Expressed conclusion.)

If after testing each argument by means of the rules for a valid syllogism all the syllogisms are found to be valid, then the sorites is valid.

CONCLUSION

Before we conclude this chapter it might be profitable to see how the tools of logic can be applied to really complex arguments. For example, how would the logic of the following argument from Augustine's *City of God* be evaluated:

The Greeks think they justly honour players, because they worship the gods who demand plays: the Romans, on the other hand, do not suffer an actor to disgrace by his name his own plebeian tribe, far less the senatorial order. And the whole of this discussion may be summed up in the following syllogism. The Greeks give us the . . . premise:

If such gods are to be worshipped, then certainly such men may be honoured. The Romans add the [other]: But such men must by no means be honoured. The Christians draw the conclusion: Therefore such gods must by no means be [worshipped].

Fortunately, Augustine himself tells us what his premises and conclusion are. Thus his first premise is: "If such gods are to be worshipped, then certainly such men may be honoured." This "if-then" sentence can be translated into one of the logical forms without too much difficulty. The sentence states that the worshiping of the (Greek) gods implies, or means, that such men (the actors) should also be honored. In short, the first premise states that all who can worship such Greek gods should honor such Greek actors. This statement is equivalent to "All who can worship such gods are ones who should honor such actors," that is, "All X is Y."

The second premise undergoes a similar translation. It becomes "No one should honour such men (actors)." This sentence, in turn, is equivalent to "No person is one who should honour such men," that is, "No Z is Y."

The conclusion then undergoes its transformation into "No person is one who can worship such gods," that is, "No Z is X."

In symbolic form the argument is:

> All X is Y
> No Z is Y
> Therefore, no Z is X.

Since the argument satisfies all the distribution rules it is valid.

Now let us examine an argument that is a little more complicated than Augustine's.

> Then, I remember, I maintain in my article that all . . . well, legislators and leaders of men, such as Lycurgus, Solon, Mahomet, Napoleon, and so on, were all without exception criminals, from the very fact that, making a new law, they transgressed the ancient one, handed down from their ancestors and held sacred by the people, and they did

not stop short at bloodshed either, if that bloodshed—often of innocent persons fighting bravely in defence of ancient law—were of use to their cause. It's remarkable, in fact, that the majority, indeed, of these benefactors and leaders of humanity were guilty of terrible carnage. In short, I maintain that all great men or even men a little out of the common, that is to say capable of giving some new word, must from their very nature be criminals—more or less, of course. Otherwise it's hard for them to get out of the common rut; and to remain in the common rut is what they can't submit to, from their very nature again, and to my mind they ought not, indeed, to submit to it. You see that there is nothing particularly new in all that. The same thing has been printed and read a thousand times before. (Dostoyevsky, *Crime and Punishment*.)

How is the logic of the argument to be evaluated? Probably the best way to begin is to discover what Dostoyevsky (or, more precisely, Raskolnikov, the hero of *Crime and Punishment*) is trying to prove. It should be apparent that Raskolnikov is arguing one primary thesis: the truly great man must be allowed to break the law. This is the conclusion of the argument. In Raskolnikov's words "They (all great men) ought not indeed to submit to it (to remain in the common rut)." This sentence must now be translated into a logical statement, which at first might appear to be of the universal-affirmative type. Although Raskolnikov does refer to "all great men," the sentence states "all great men ought not . . ." and we have no logical statement such as "All X is *not* Y." However, the statement "All X is *not* Y" is clearly equivalent to "No X is Y"—"No great man is one who ought to submit to remaining in the common rut." The conclusion is universal-negative.

If this is the conclusion, what are the premises, the reasons Raskolnikov gives for justifying his conclusion? Raskolnikov gives one main reason—"All great men . . . must from their very nature be criminals," a statement he supports by citing the examples of Lycurgus, Solon, Mahomet, Napoleon, and so on. Thus, the argument is an enthymeme:

All great men are people who must from their very nature
be criminals. (All X is Z.)
Therefore, no great man is one who ought to submit to
remaining in the common rut. (No X is Y.)

Since this argument is an enthymeme it cannot be evaluated
until the missing premise is discovered. But how are we to discover this premise? Sometimes a hidden premise (or conclusion) is made explicit as we continue to read further. Or the
premise may be supplied from other sources of information. For
example, Dostoyevsky's concept of Raskolnikov's character may
be ascertained from other writings, so that it may be possible
to test the validity of the argument. But here Dostoyevsky's
Raskolnikov may be given the "benefit of the doubt" and the
premise supplied that makes an enthymeme of the following
form valid:

> All Y is Z
> ?
> Therefore, no X is Y.

The fourth rule of the valid syllogism states that if the conclusion is negative then at least one premise must be negative.
Thus the missing premise must be negative. The rules also
require that the middle term must appear in both premises
and not in the conclusion. Thus Z and not X must be the middle term. The other term must be Y, since there must be three
terms in the premises of a syllogism. As a result we now know
that the missing premise must be one of the following:

> 1) Some Z is not Y.
> 2) Some Y is not Z.
> 3) No Z is Y
> 4) No Y is Z.

It cannot be (1), since this would violate the rule concerning
the distribution of the middle term, Z, which is also undistributed in the first premise. It cannot be (2), since Y is undistributed, but it is distributed in the conclusion, "No X is Y,"
thus violating the rule that distributed terms in the conclusion

must be distributed in the premises. However, (3) or (4) would make the syllogism valid: "No people who must by their very nature be criminals are ones who ought to submit to remaining in the common rut" or vice versa. Raskolnikov's argument implicitly assumes this premise. Probably Raskolnikov himself was unaware of such implicit premises. In fact, frequently illogical arguments seem to be logical because the implicit premises are never made explicit.

Although Raskolnikov's reasoning has been formulated as a valid syllogism, it should be remembered that validity is not truth. Raskolnikov's argument may be valid, but it may also be false. Ideally, an argument should be *both* valid and true. If either one of these characteristics is missing, then the argument is defective. Thus, Raskolnikov's argument may be attacked on the grounds that his implicit premise is really false. And if it is false, then his conclusion can also be false. It is important to remember that a conclusion is necessarily true only if the argument is valid and the premises are true. A false premise may not invalidate the argument, but it destroys the guarantee that the conclusion must be true.

EXERCISES

Test the following arguments for validity, indicating whether the argument is a syllogism, enthymeme, or sorites.

(1) As everyone knows, except the dupes and fellow travelers, Communists are staunch defenders of socialized medicine and strong unions. Similarly, the Democratic party is in the vanguard of the propaganda for socialized medicine and strong unions. The implications I need not draw for this intelligent audience.

(2) Anyone who has the best interest of the United States at heart will fight against communism. Senator X is a tireless fighter against communism. Senator X can stand on his record as one who has the best interests of America at heart.

(3) There is no one who wants to leave his loved one and go off to war. But voting for my political opponent means that war will surely come. Do not vote for my opponent.

(4) Only syllogisms which conform to rules are valid. This syllogism conforms to the rules. This syllogism is valid.

(5) All syllogisms containing only two premises are fallacious. This syllogism does not contain two premises. Therefore this syllogism is not fallacious.

(6) Because it's crystal clear . . . there's no gin like Gordon's.

(7) The new cereal treat! Healthos! Now we can all have rugged health.

(8) Ask the man who owns one!

(9) No other traitorous party but the Communist Party is a danger to the United States. A danger to the United States should be exposed. I think we can support those who are exposing Communists.

(10) None but the lonely heart can know my grief. Jane has a lonely heart. Jane can know my grief.

(11) The Democrats are pro-union, as everybody recognizes. And experience teaches us that pro-union groups tend toward communistic doctrines. Groups that have this tendency can be disastrous to our country. Democrats can be disastrous to our country.

(12) Knowing more than one language is helpful to the serious writer. For knowledge of languages shows that the same idea may be expressed by different words. We are thus enabled to discriminate between words and ideas. This is important to clear thinking.

(13) Dale Carnegie has shown that the way to make friends is to appear to be interested in them. But the way to appear interested is to be interested. To be interested in others we must cease to be self-centered.

(14) (In Boethius' *Consolation of Philosophy*, Book 2, Prose 12, appears an argument for the nonexistence of evil which may be loosely paraphrased.) God is the Creator of all that exists. Since God is good, what He creates is good. But since no evil is good, no evil exists. It follows that evil is nonexistent.

(15) There was, for example, the explanation of evil in terms of economic inequality and injustice. Socialist writers had taught my generation that bad conditions were the cause of human wretchedness; of human wretchedness and also of human wickedness.

And the moral? That evil is due to bad social conditions. Now you can reform bad social conditions by Act of Parliament, substituting comfort, cleanliness, security and financial competence for discomfort, dirt, insecurity and want. Therefore, presumably, you can make men virtuous, or at any rate as nearly virtuous as makes no matter, by Act of Parliament. (C. E. M. Joad, *Good and Evil.*)

(16) Again, trade is a social act. Whoever undertakes to sell any description of goods to the public does what affects the interest of other persons, and of society in general; and thus his conduct, in principle, comes within the jurisdiction of society . . . . (J. S. Mill, *On Liberty.*)

(17) If death, said my father, reasoning with himself, is nothing but the separation of the soul from the body; and if it is true that people can walk about and do their business without brains—then certes the soul does not inhabit there. (L. Sterne, *Tristram Shandy.*)

(18) Since everything is knowable according as it is actual, God, who is pure act, without any admixture of potentiality, is in Himself supremely knowable. But what is supremely knowable in itself may not be knowable to a particular intellect, because of the excess of the intelligible object above the intellect; as for example, the sun, which is supremely visible, cannot be seen by the bat by reason of its excess of light. (N.B. The *conclusion* must be supplied.) (St. Thomas Aquinas, *Summa*

Theologica, Question XII, First Article, Objection 4, English
Dominican translation, amended by Pegis.)

(19) [Since] political capacity is innate in man, and is to be
further developed, it is quite inaccurate to call the State a
necessary evil. We have to deal with it as a lofty necessity of
Nature. (H. von Treitschke, *Politics*, translated by Dugdale
and de Bille.)

(20) There is no concept of the State which is not funda-
mentally a concept of life: philosophy or intuition, a system of
ideas which develops logically or is gathered up into a vision or
into a faith, but which is always, at least virtually, an organic
conception of the world.
Thus Fascism could not be understood in many of its practical manifestations as a party organization, as a system of education, as a discipline, if it were not always looked at in the
light of its whole way of conceiving life, a spiritualized way.
(Benito Mussolini in the *Italian Encyclopedia*, quoted by Oakeshott, *The Social and Political Doctrines of Contemporary Europe*.)

(21) Further, if the passing of slow quantitative changes into
rapid and abrupt qualitative changes is a law of development,
then it is clear that revolutions made by oppressed classes are
a quite natural and inevitable phenomenon. (Joseph Stalin,
Dialectical and Historical Materialism.)

(22) We have already said, in the first part of this treatise,
when discussing household management and the rule of the
master, that man is by nature a political animal. And, therefore,
men, even when they do not require one another's help, desire
to live together. . . . (Aristotle, *Politics* III 5, translated by
W. D. Ross.)

(23) In bourgeois society, living labor is but a means to increase accumulated labor. In Communist society, accumulated
labor is but a means to widen, to enrich, to promote the existence of the laborer. In bourgeois society, therefore, the past
dominates the present; in Communist society, the present domi-

nates the past. In bourgeois society, capital is independent and has individuality, while the living person is dependent and has no individuality. (Marx and Engels, *The Communist Manifesto*.)

(24) It may be objected, "But *some* received principles, especially on the highest and most vital subjects, are more than half-truths. The Christian morality, for instance, is the whole truth on that subject, and if anyone teaches a morality which varies from it, he is wholly in error." (J. S. Mill, *On Liberty*.)

(25) The human soul is a thing whose activity is thinking; a thing whose activity is thinking is one whose activity is immediately apprehended, and without any representation of parts therein. A thing whose activity is apprehended immediately without any representation of parts therein, is a thing whose activity does not contain parts. A thing whose activity does not contain parts is one whose activity is motion, for all motion is divisible into parts. A thing whose activity is not motion is not a body, for the activity of a body is always a motion. What is not a body is not in space: for the definition of body is to be extended. What is not in space is insusceptible of motion. What is insusceptible of motion is indissoluble: for dissolution is a movement of parts. What is indissoluble is incorruptible: for corruption is dissolution of the inmost parts. What is incorruptible is immortal. Therefore the human soul is immortal. (Leibniz, *Confessio Naturae contra Atheistas*, translated by Joseph, *An Introduction to Logic*.)

(26) Dostoyevsky said, "If God didn't exist everything would be possible." That is the very starting point of existentialism. Indeed, everything is permissible if God does not exist, and as a result man is forlorn, because neither within him nor without does he find anything to cling to. He can't start making excuses for himself. If God does not exist, we find no values or commands to turn to which legitimize our conduct. So, in the bright realm of values, we have no excuses behind us, nor justification before us. (Jean-Paul Sartre, *Existentialism*.)

(27) ". . . men are in general divided by a law of nature into two categories, inferior (ordinary), that is, so to say, material that serves only to reproduce its kind, and men who have the gift or the talent to utter *a new word* . . . The first category, generally speaking, are men conservative in temperament and law-abiding; they live under control and love to be controlled. To my thinking it is their duty to be controlled, because that's their vocation, and there is nothing humiliating in it for them. The second category all transgress the law; they are destroyers or disposed to destruction according to their capacities . . . if such a one is forced for the sake of his idea to step over a corpse or wade through blood, he can, I maintain, find within himself, in his conscience, a sanction for wading through blood. . . ." (Raskolnikov in Dosteyevsky, *Crime and Punishment.*)

(28) What is honor? A word. What is in that word honor? What is that honor? Air. A trim reckoning! Who hath it? He that died o' Wednesday. Doth he feel it? No. Doth he hear it? No. 'Tis insensible, then? Yea, to the dead. But will it not live with the living? No. Why? Detraction will not suffer it. Therefore I'll none of it; Honor is a mere scutcheon. (Shakespeare, *Henry the Fourth.*)

APPENDIX TO CHAPTER 4: A SYSTEM OF DIAGRAMS

Although distribution rules are an important means of testing the validity of an argument, another—more pictorial—means can be employed—the diagram.

The diagram uses two overlapping circles which represent the symbols X and Y respectively:

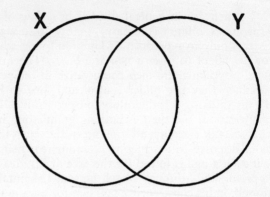

"All X is Y" is represented as follows:

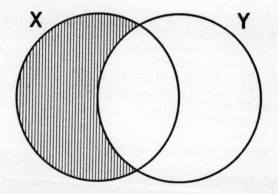

This diagram pictures the relationship expressed by "All X is Y." "All X is Y" states that all of X is included in Y. Thus any X which is not included in Y is to be eliminated. This is indicated by blackening all of the X circle which does not fall within the Y circle.

To diagram "No X is Y" two overlapping circles are drawn, but this time everything which X and Y have in common is blacked out.

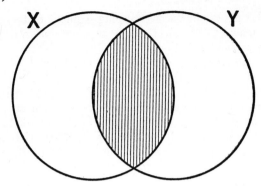

This diagram reveals that no X is included in any part of Y, exactly the information to be found in the statement "No X is Y."

A different problem arises when a particular affirmative or a particular negative is diagrammed. In "Some X is Y" nothing is said about X's being excluded from Y or vice versa. It merely states that X and Y overlap, and that the overlapping portion is not empty, that is, one or more of X also belongs to Y. Logicians symbolize this relationship by means of the following diagram:

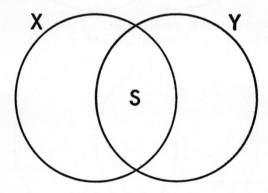

The form "Some X is Y" informs us that there are *some existent things* which are both X's and Y's, that is, that both

X's and Y's appear in the overlapping segment of the diagram. The "S" placed in the overlapping segment indicates that existent things belong both to X and Y.

The particular negative "Some X is not Y" states that some X things exist and that these X things are not Y's. The form does *not* tell us that all X's are excluded from Y, but only that X contains one or more existent members which are *not* Y's. In other words, the form tells us only that some of the members of X exist and are not part of Y. This relationship is diagrammed by placing "S" in the segment of X which is excluded from Y in the overlapping circles:

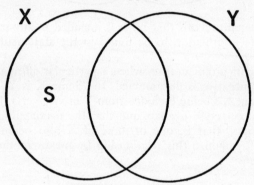

These results can be summarized:
All X is Y   Universal Affirmative

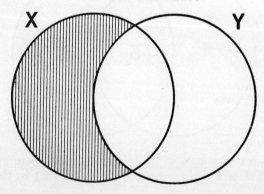

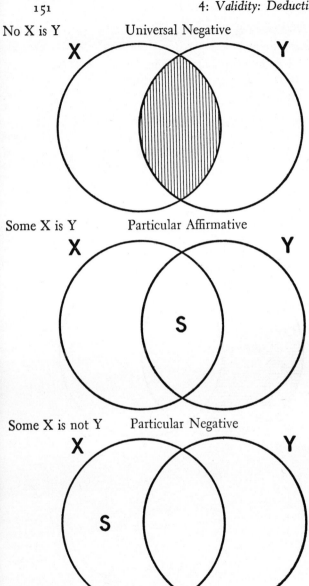

No X is Y   Universal Negative

Some X is Y   Particular Affirmative

Some X is not Y   Particular Negative

The procedures listed above may now be applied to the logical analysis of an argument such as the following:

> All college students are intelligent persons.
> No intelligent person is a criminal.
> Therefore, no criminal is a college student.

We now substitute X's, Y's, and Z's for the particular subjects and predicates. X is substituted for "college students," Y for "intelligent persons," and Z for "criminals." The first premise is a universal affirmative, with the form "All X is Y." Similarly, the second premise is a universal negative with the form "No Y is Z." The conclusion is also a universal negative, with the form "No X is Z." As a result the argument yields the following set of equations:

Universal Affirmative: All X is Y

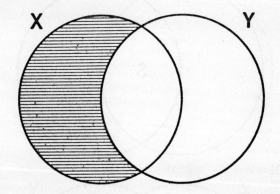

Universal Negative: No Y is Z

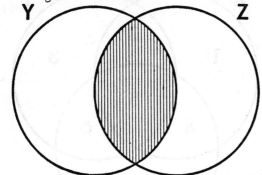

Therefore, Universal Negative: No X is Z

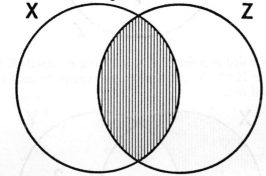

These forms and the circle diagrams which represent them are the only tools required for testing the logical validity of an argument. By manipulating these tools in accordance with some very simple rules, the validity of any argument can immediately be checked in the following manner. First draw three circles, each overlapping the other, and with each of the resulting compartments numbered. Each circle represents the three symbols involved in the premises of a syllogism. But just as circles can be used to diagram the relationship between *two* terms, similarly circles can diagram the relationship between *three* terms. The three-circle diagram is drawn in the following way:

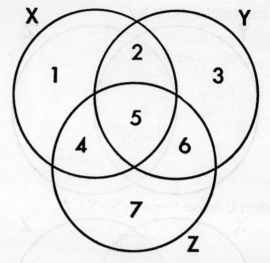

Since the first premise "All X is Y" is a universal-affirmative, only circles X and Y are involved and compartments 1 and 4 are blocked out.

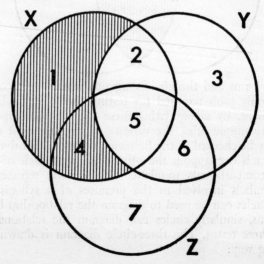

In our second premise, "No Y is Z," we are concerned only with Y and Z. Since this premise is a universal-negative we block out compartments 5 and 6:

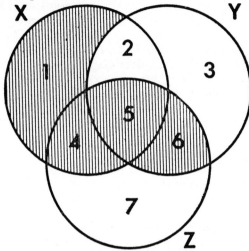

The conclusion of the syllogism is "No Y is Z." The single diagram for the two premises tells us that compartments 4 and 5 have been blocked out. Examination shows that with compartments 4 and 5 blocked out the diagram requirements have been satisfied for the form, "No X is Z":

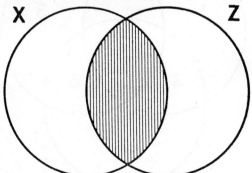

Therefore the conclusion is logically correct.

The argument is shown to be valid. *Whenever the conclusion of a syllogism becomes diagrammed in the process of diagramming the premises, then the syllogism will always be valid.* On the other hand, had there been two premises from which only 4 or 5 had been blocked out, the conclusion would have been invalid. Only if 4 and 5 are *both* blocked out is "No X is Z" logically valid. Remember: *Only the two premises are diagrammed; the conclusion is never diagrammed.* The conclusion, to follow logically from the premises, is determined by diagramming the premises. If the conclusion is not diagrammed by the two premises then the argument is invalid.

Consider the following syllogism which seems to make sense:

All students are eager to learn	All X is Y
All hard workers are eager to learn	All Z is Y
Therefore all students are	
hard workers	Therefore all Z is X

Does the conclusion follow logically?
First of all draw the basic three-circle diagram:

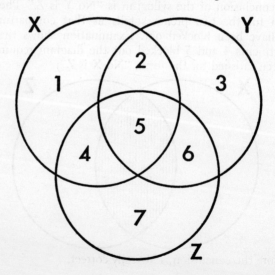

The first premise is in the form "All X is Y" so that compartments 1 and 4 must be blocked out. The second premise, also a universal affirmative, "All Z is Y," requires us to block out 7 and 4. We are left then with the following result:

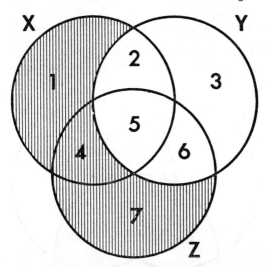

The conclusion "All Z is X" requires that compartments 6 and 7 be already blocked out. Compartment 7 is blocked out, *but 6 is not.* Only if both 6 and 7 were blocked out would it have been legitimate to say that all Z is included in X. Thus the syllogism is not valid. It may seem to make good sense, but the conclusion does not follow logically from the premises. In fact, the lack of validity is demonstrable in perhaps a more obvious way. It is impossible for a syllogism to be valid and also have two true premises and a false conclusion. But it is easy to think of an argument that employs the same logical form and has two true premises with a false conclusion. For example:

Kangaroos are animals	All X is Y
Cats are animals	All Z is Y
Therefore cats are kangaroos	Therefore all Z is X

The two premises are true, but the conclusion is obviously false.

Is the following syllogism valid?

No cats are kangaroos	No X is Y
No mice are kangaroos	No Z is Y
Therefore some cats are not mice	Therefore some X is not Z

The first premise tells us to block out 2 and 5. The second premise tells us to block out 5 and 6. The completed diagram would be:

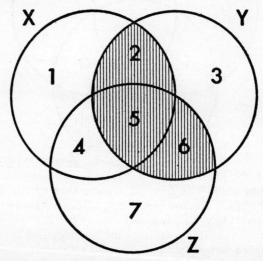

At first glance the conclusion "Some X is not Z" would seem to be justified. Compartment 1 is not blocked out, nor is it included in compartment 7. But if we refer back to the diagram for the particular negative, we find it to be:

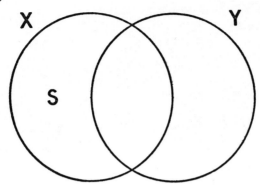

Since the diagram lacks the "S" in compartment 1 we are not justified in drawing the conclusion "Some X is not Z." We can also again appeal to "common sense." If our syllogism is legitimate then true premises should lead to a true conclusion. But it is obvious that we can use the same symbolic form to obtain a syllogism with true premises and a false conclusion. For example:

No horses are fish	No X is Y
No animals are fish	No Z is Y
Therefore some horses are not animals	Therefore some X is not Z

Let us examine still another syllogism:

All scholars are seekers of truth	All X is Y
All seekers of truth are tolerant men	All Y is Z
Therefore all scholars are tolerant men	Therefore all X is Z

Is this syllogism valid? Our final diagram for this would be:

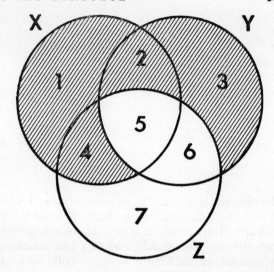

Since all that is left of X (viz., that which is in compartment 5) is completely included in Z, the syllogism is valid. The conclusion logically follows from the premises.

Assuming the above syllogism to be valid, can we also draw the conclusion "Some X is Z"? At first glance it might seem as if we should be permitted to draw this conclusion. If all apples are red, then it should be obvious that some apples are also red. And if all the students in this classroom are male, then it should also be permissible to assert that some of them are male. But strictly speaking we are not permitted to go from a universal affirmative to a particular affirmative. A particular conclusion cannot be obtained from two universal premises. Universal statements do not have the "S" sign that is required for the particular statement. Moreover, the form "Some X is Y" refers to the fact that there are *existent things* in the group consisting of X and Y. When we say "Some buffaloes are furry" we mean that there are some individual things which are furry buffaloes. On the other hand, when we say "All buffaloes are furry" we simply mean that *if* there are buffaloes, they are all furry. We need not be certain that any buffaloes exist. The universal affirmative does not guarantee that its subject has any actual members in

it. Thus to say "All X is Y" does not imply that there actually
are some X's in existence. To say "All unicorns are horned"
does not mean that there actually are unicorns which exist.
Before we can go from a universal affirmative or negative to a
particular affirmative or negative we must make sure that the
universal statements refer to groups having existent members.
Without such information, which makes possible the employment of the "S" symbol, we have no right to go from universal
to particular. Logic teaches us not to "jump to conclusions."

Let us examine one final example:

Some officers are in the Army	Some X is Y
Some men are not in the Army	Some Z is not Y
Therefore some officers are not men	Some X is not Z

Since the first premise is a particular affirmative, "S" is placed
directly on the line separating compartments 2 and 5. This is
done because we do not know whether the members of X are
in 2, 5, or in both. Similarly the second premise tells us to
place "S" on the line separating 4 and 7, since we do not know
whether the members of Z are in 4, 7, or in both. The following
diagram results:

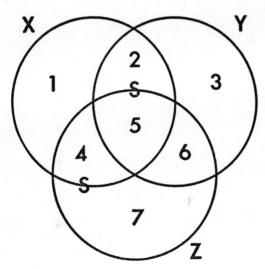

If the conclusion logically follows, then an "S" would have to appear either in 1 or 2, or on the line separating them. But since the premises do not tell us whether the "S" between 2 and 5 actually belongs in either 2 or 5, we cannot assume that the "S" is in 2. Therefore, this syllogism is invalid.

RECOMMENDED READINGS

Lionel Ruby, *Logic*. (Philadelphia: J. B. Lippincott Co., 1950) Chapters 7, 8, 9, 10.

Max Black, *Critical Thinking*. Second edition. (New York: Prentice-Hall, 1952) Chapters 2, 3, 8.

Irving M. Copi, *Introduction to Logic*. (New York: The Macmillan Co., 1953) Chapters 5, 6, 7.

Morris R. Cohen and Ernest Nagel, *Logic and Scientific Method*. (New York: Harcourt, Brace & Co., 1934) Chapter 4.

RELIABILITY: INDUCTIVE LOGIC

VALIDITY AND RELIABILITY

DEDUCTIVE logic is primarily concerned with the relationship between premises and conclusion. Logicians, like mathematicians, seek to answer one important question: Given certain premises, what conclusion follows from them? The premises may actually be false, such as "All women are cowards" and "All cowards are males." But it would be perfectly logical to conclude from these premises, "Therefore, all women are males." The conclusion is false but logical. Similarly, the following is a valid syllogism:

> All mome raths are borogoves.
> All borogoves are jabberwockies.
> Therefore all mome raths are jabberwockies.

Unfortunately, premises are rarely so presented that their absurdity or falsity is immediately recognizable. As a result people have often confused *logical* conclusions with *trustworthy* or *reliable* conclusions. Plato's argument against democracy may be translated into the following syllogism:

All democracies are ruled by illiterates.
All countries ruled by illiterates deteriorate into tyrannies.
Therefore all democracies deteriorate into tyrannies.

But in spite of the false premise, "All democracies are ruled by illiterates," Plato's argument has been accepted by many as both logical and true. But if either one of the premises of an argument is false or even questionable then no amount of deductive logic can guarantee the truth of the conclusion. For this reason the best kind of argument depends upon both logical relationships and reliable premises. Inductive logic concerns the means of attaining reliable beliefs.

The discovery of reliable premises is not an easy task. Beliefs have been considered reliable for the most superficial reasons. Very often people believe something simply because they have always believed it, and they become unhappy when they are told that their beliefs are false. Sometimes they believe something because "authority" tells them to believe it. For this reason they often refer to others to support their views: "How do you know?" "Oh, *we all* believe that. *Everybody* knows that." Finally they tend to believe in something, without checking its reliability, because they "feel it in their bones," or because "something deep inside" tells them it is true. But what people "always" believed, what "everybody" knew, what they felt "deep in their bones," may be false in the present and have no meaning for subsequent generations. Not very long ago everybody knew and had known for thousands of years that the sun revolves around the earth and that there were four, and only four, elements.

One of the best ways to obtain reliable information is to insist that statements be verifiable. Instead of believing something because "someone in the know" told us, or because "everybody knows it's so," we must devise a way of testing whereby anyone can determine for himself whether or not the statement coincides with some actual state of affairs. When a statement has been verified, it is *reliable*.

When verification is employed as a standard for reliability, certain drawbacks are involved. First, *truth* becomes more an ideal *to be* attained rather than one that has been attained. Instead of working with *true* statements, that is, statements that cannot be wrong, we must be satisfied with *reliable* statements, that is, statements that may turn out to be false as more and more information is accumulated. Second, the comforting sense of certainty that accompanies the "feeling" that something has "got" to be true is replaced by the not-so-comforting awareness that our beliefs are only *probable* and always tentative. In demanding that a belief be verified, we must accept the possibility that it may be wrong. More than that, even if one test confirms it, the possibility remains that another test in the future may prove it false. Thus, accepting verification as a criterion means that all beliefs are at best probable and tentative. But all knowledge is not therefore condemned to the ashes. The main problem for thinking human beings is to obtain probable and thus reliable beliefs. There are degrees of probability. When we seek to verify beliefs, we seek for what is most probable. Both Ptolemy's and Copernicus's theories of the universe were probable, but Copernicus's theory is accepted because of its higher degree of probability. We should try to find the best and most probable beliefs, even though they can still be wrong.

One of the ways in which a statement can be tested is to make use of sense observation. For example, if we say, "There is a desk in the next room," we can actually go and see the desk in the next room. If we are unsure of our own vision or of our memory, we can call on others for verification. If others also see the desk in the room, our belief is highly probable—but, even so, only probable. There remains the possibility, however slight, that what is taken to be a desk may actually be something else. But for all practical purposes our information is reliable if everyone we invite to verify our belief insists that he sees a desk in the other room.

A statement like the above about a single object can be easily verified. We need only to be sure that there are observers other than ourselves and that these observers are competent and unbiased. If a desk exists in the other room, it will appear as an object with certain properties, a writing surface, drawers, legs, etc. If these properties are reported as belonging to the object, we have sufficient verification to give us practical, although not absolute, certainty. But our difficulties increase as we move from a statement about a single instance to a statement about many instances, that is, as we *generalize*. The reliability of a *generali-*

zation cannot be established by observation of a single instance because a generalization states that all objects of a certain kind have some specific characteristic, or set of characteristics. "All metals are conductors," "All men are mortal," "All pennies are forms of currency" are generalizations. They claim that all objects of a given group have given characteristics.

EXERCISES

Do you consider your belief or lack of belief in each of the following reliable? Explain what your belief is based upon.
1. The earth is round.
2. The sun will rise every morning.
3. The sun revolves around the earth.
4. There is a dark side to the moon.
5. Everything is made up of atoms.
6. $2 + 2 = 4$.
7. Man is naturally good.
8. "Ain't" is bad grammar.
9. "It's me" is bad grammar.
10. Shakespeare wrote *Hamlet, Othello,* and many other famous plays.

UNRELIABLE GENERALIZATIONS

Generalizations are the most important tools in gaining knowledge. If we were unable to group things in the present and assert that things like them in the future will have similar properties, we could never make a prediction. Every object called a metal would require a new test for its conductivity. It is by virtue of generalization that the most important kinds of knowledge are described. Thus the basic problem is *how to obtain reliable generalizations.*

Emotive Generalizations. Generalizations, like other kinds of human belief, are usually specious. People are always ready to say, "All people are this" or "All people are that." Yet the evidence for their opinions often ranges from the absurd to the fantastic. Political speakers can appeal to audiences with such statements as "Americans are brave," or "Americans are loyal." Such generalizations are based on little more than patriotic feelings of self-approval. Indeed, emotional stress frequently leads to generalization. We are led by momentary emotion to admonish or to encourage others by means of generalizations as the father does when he says to his son, "Don't hit Susie. No gentleman ever strikes a lady." In moments of anger women call men fools and men call women gold-diggers. Such universal statements as these can be termed *emotive generalizations*. They tell us only how a person feels or how he wants his audience to feel. They cannot be considered reliable—except as an index to the feelings of the speaker.

Subjective Generalizations. On the other hand, many generalizations are based on more than mere emotion. Yet giving the reasons for a belief is not always tantamount to insuring that it is reliable. We might maintain that all Americans are brave *because* we observed them fighting the Nazis. This generalization does at least depend upon some reason which vouches for its reliability. Nevertheless, this universal statement is far from reliable. What to one man may be an instance of bravery may be to another an instance of foolhardiness or stupidity. One piece of evidence is frequently contradicted by another. Generalizations of this kind are called *subjective generalizations*. They are based on evidence, but evidence so purely personal as to have little weight. Their verification involves nothing but appeal to such incidents in our experience which tend to support them. No attempt is made to analyze the evidence or to consider the views of others. Thus little reliance may be placed on subjective generalizations.

Popular Generalizations. The deficiencies of the subjective generalization suggest a possible remedy. Perhaps if we could show that the statement "All Americans are brave" is universally affirmed, then the statement would seem to be verified. Not the

individual alone, but everyone vouches for the statement. This
kind of generalization, the *popular generalization*, seems to be
satisfactory. One individual could be wrong, but certainly not
everyone could be wrong: "160 million Americans can't be
wrong." But before the popular generalization can be evaluated,
certain facts must be established. First of all, the word *everyone*
does not literally mean *everyone*, since we cannot ask what
everyone feels. Furthermore, *everyone* sometimes is only a substitute for *I*. When we feel something strongly we tend to talk ourselves into believing that everyone else must feel the same
way we do. But if *everyone* is a projection of ourselves, we are
simply disguising a subjective generalization as a popular one.
To be meaningful *everyone* must refer to many or at least some
people who believe as we do. But the fact that others believe
what we do does not make our views reliable. Whole nations
have been prejudiced and have acted blindly. Very often one
man and not the great majority has been right and has given
to mankind its greatest moral, religious, and scientific truths.
Therefore, popular generalizations must also be considered unreliable, although, as will be shown, *when other conditions are
fulfilled*, popular generalizations can produce reliability.

EXERCISES

*Of the following statements check those you consider to be
generalizations. Indicate for each generalization its type: (1)
emotive, (2) subjective, (3) popular.*

(1) I'm all alone by the telephone.
(2) Dogs are man's best friends.
(3) I've never seen it fail—a woman driver!
(4) My dog has fleas.
(5) My country right or wrong!
(6) You all better go home.
(7) The land of the free and the home of the brave.
(8) No gentleman eats peas with a knife.
(9) Why, the way she treats her boy friend—it just isn't
human.

(10) Those utility companies are all alike—heartless—a few days late with your bill and off go the lights.

All of the preceding kinds of generalizations are based primarily on feelings and emotions. People make such generalizations because they want to believe them and find comfort in the assurance which such statements bring them. But emotive, subjective, and popular generalizations *are not reliable*. The criterion for reliable generalizations is still to be found.

Definitory Generalizations. Reliable generalizations are not based on the whims and fantasies of human feelings. Although human beings are emotional and subjective in their responses, they can make nonsubjective, nonemotive generalizations. For example, the statement "A penny is a form of currency having an exchange value in ratio to other currency" is a generalization, but it is clearly not one we believe in because it "feels right" to us, or even because our friends believe in it. On the contrary, to substantiate it we would refer to something other than our personal feelings. If we were asked why we believed this statement about pennies, we would appeal to the law of the land, the law which makes commerce possible. The law governing currency makes it mandatory for us to speak of the penny in a given way. Our personal likes and dislikes in this matter do not add or detract from the reliability of the generalization. It is reliable because it is derived from a body of laws by which an entire nation (*everyone*) is governed. Such a generalization is called a *definitory generalization*. Definitory generalizations are stipulations, or arbitrary agreements that anything having a certain name is to be regarded in a given way. We, as members of a society, agree to the arbitrary stipulation that the word "penny" is to be defined as a form of currency. Thus if an object is called a "penny" then it will be considered a form of currency. *A definitory generalization is about a word, not about what the word signifies.* Even if there were no actual pennies in existence, the definitory generalization would hold for the word "penny" because the reliability of the generalization is dependent solely on a man-made rule to use words in a certain way. However, there are times when we actually speak about the object represented by the word "penny." If we say "pennies are copper" we are describing characteristics that pennies actually *seem to have*. But a thing may be a penny and still not be copper. (During the war many pennies were of noncopper alloy.) A definitory generalization is not tested by experience or experiment, but by some set of language rules accepted by the community. From the accepted meaning of the word "bachelor" we know that the definitory generalization "All bachelors are unmarried men" is reliable. Similarly, if we know the meaning of the word "effect," then we know that the statement "Every effect must have a cause" is reliable. We arbitrarily agree to define such words as "bachelor" and "effect" in specific ways.

Scientific Generalizations. However, most generalizations do not refer simply to the meaning of words. The most useful generalizations are assertions about the world we live in. The statements "All bodies act in accordance with the law of gravitation" or "All metals are tensile" do not merely define words. They are actually saying that we believe the world to be so constituted that all objects are subject to gravitation and all metals are tensile. Such views are not based upon subjective feelings. On the contrary, they are based upon some series of tests and experiments which anyone, regardless of his bias or his feelings, is capable of performing. Generalizations based upon tests and experiment may be called *scientific generalizations*.

Since a scientific generalization is based upon experimentation and since experiment can always reveal a belief to be wrong, a *scientific generalization is corrigible,* i.e., it is always capable of being proved wrong. No scientific generalization is so foolproof that it can never be wrong. Newton's theories had to be modified in the light of new evidence for which Einstein's theories alone accounted. Nor are Einstein's theories of relativity incapable of being proved wrong. History gives us many examples of so-called absolute (i.e., unfalsifiable) laws which have turned out to be wrong. In fact, we should be wary of any theories about the world, society, or individuals which claim to be unfalsifiable. The Marxist theory of social evolution maintains that society *must necessarily* evolve in such a way that capitalism finally gives way to communism. The law is so stated that regardless of what men do and what events occur, the law is always right. Because of the claim that Marxist law can never be wrong, it is not acceptable as a genuine scientific generalization.

However, we need not jump to the conclusion that a scientific generalization must be based upon a study of every object specified by it. When we state that all metals are tensile, we do not mean that every piece of metal has actually been tested. But if we admit that we have not tested every object, how can we claim reliability for the scientific generalization?

To answer this question we must distinguish between two kinds of scientific generalizations: (1) enumerative, (2) hypothetical.

Enumeration. The *enumerative generalization* is a generalization based on the *number* of past occurrences of a given kind. Thus the statement "All metals unite with oxygen to form oxides" is considered reliable because in the past a great number of metals have been found under proper conditions to unite with oxygen and form oxides. The experimental fact behind the generalization does not guarantee that all metals will have this property. But, since it would be impossible to check each individual metal substance in the universe, we do say that what holds for a given number of tested cases will also hold for all other untested cases. Usually when a generalization is supported by a great number of tests, the probability is high that further tests will tend to support it. But no matter how large a sample is obtained, an *inductive leap* must be made—the leap from knowledge about a part to knowledge about the whole.

Enumerative generalizations are frequently of two kinds: uniform and statistical. A *uniform enumerative generalization* is one which leads from a specific number of cases to a generalization about all similar cases. Thus if fifty redheaded persons were found to be temperamental, we might predict that all redheaded persons are temperamental. On the other hand, a *statistical enumerative generalization* is concerned with *percentage*. For example, we might discover that 75 per cent of a thousand redheaded persons were temperamental. If another thousand redheaded persons were examined and 75 per cent of them were discovered to be temperamental, we could assert that 75 per cent of all redheaded persons are temperamental. Note first of all that we are assuming a connection between redheadedness and temperament. This connection may be fortuitous. In fact, the temperament of the groups examined may be controlled by another factor such as glands and not the factor of redheadedness.

Furthermore, statistical generalizations can be made concerning events that actually have no connection at all to one another. Thus, correlations have been made between the spread of cancer and the increased importation of apples, the increase of teachers' salaries and the retail price of beer, the average salaries of Presbyterian ministers in Massachusetts and the price of rum in Havana, Cuba, and the increased enrollments in colleges and the increased enrollments in insane asylums. Moreover, just as we make the inductive leap, the leap from *some* to *all* in a uniform enumerative generalization, similarly we make the inductive leap in a statistical enumerative generalization when we asume that the percentage found in *some* samples in a group is actually the percentage of the group as a whole. In a uniform enumerative generalization, the larger the number of cases which make up the selection usually the higher the degree of probability. In a statistical enumerative generalization, the greater the number of samples, the more reliable the generalization.

Generalizations based upon enumeration, whether uniform or statistical, can often be misleading. In a test of an indefinite number of objects any sample with certain characteristics may not be representative; it may not be a true sample at all. The famous Gallup poll which predicted Truman's defeat in his race against Thomas Dewey illustrates the weaknesses and dangers inherent in any enumerative generalization. To safeguard against these weaknesses three factors must be considered whenever generalizations are based either on uniform or statistical enumeration.

1. *Probability rests upon other factors besides the mere number of cases cited.* The probability attached to a generalization is usually in ratio to the number of cases offered in support of it. Examining ten cases will not yield so good a probability as examining two hundred cases. On the other hand, the ratio between number of instances and degree of probability does not always hold. Thus the *more* times a flashlight operates, the *less* probable will it be that the flashlight will continue to operate. Against our simple enumerative generalization must be placed our knowledge of the essentials in the operation of a flashlight, that it is powered by batteries and that batteries lose power proportionately with use and age. The fact that the sun has constantly risen in the past seems to argue for its continuing to rise in the future. Yet against this enumerative generalization must be placed the information given us by astronomers who tell us that the sun is steadily losing tremendous amounts of energy. If what they tell us is true, as time passes there will be less probability that the sun will continue to rise. Thus merely accumulating numbers will not in itself guarantee reliability. Simple enumeration must be supplemented by detailed knowledge of the objects under consideration.

2. *The greater the variation among the objects sampled the larger the sample must be.* When we are trying to discover what percentage of individuals has a certain characteristic, our sampling procedure must be carefully controlled. If the individuals have many differences among themselves, we will have to select a very large sampling in order to make sure the characteristic does not occur only among certain individuals. Thus, for example, when we try to relate redheadedness to temperament we have to select a very large sample because 1) no scientific data establish a relationship between redheadedness and temperament; 2) a small group in which the two characteristics are connected might be the exception rather than the rule; and

3) all groups are not homogeneous. A given type of wheat is fairly uniform in quality, whereas the quality of peaches can vary greatly. Therefore, we feel more confident with a limited sampling of wheat than we do with a limited sampling of peaches.

The same factor of variation obviously holds true for statistical enumerative generalizations. If a new drug is tested on fifteen patients and it varies in effectiveness from 80 to 90 per cent, many more tests are required before any generalization can be made about the effectiveness of the drug. The patients may have had some particular characteristic by virtue of which they reacted positively to the drug. But this does not mean that all other patients will also react positively. The social scientist may discover that of the twenty-five college freshmen interviewed, ten have I.Q.'s of 125 and over, five have I.Q.'s of 100 to 125, and ten have I.Q.'s of 60 to 100. But he will demand a much larger survey before he begins to trust the statistical generalization "40 per cent of all college freshmen have I.Q.'s of less than 100." Forty per cent of the twenty-five selected freshmen may have low I.Q.'s, but perhaps the sample was not really representative. And if it was, perhaps it was representative only at the one particular college. The knowledge that human beings are very different causes the statistician to be very careful in his generalizing.

3. *Generalizations should be supported by substantiating evidence from other areas of inquiry.* As we have seen, the enumerative generalization must be supported by actual knowledge of the objects involved. For this reason an attempt should always be made to show that an enumerative generalization is supported by other findings besides the particular samples employed. With such information generalizations become much more reliable. For example, an enumerative generalization, "All metals are conductors," may be obtained by observing that a specific number of metals react to an electrical current. But if such observation is re-enforced by data from chemistry and physics, namely, that metals are made up of atoms which can react positively with other atoms, the generalization becomes

much more reliable. For this reason substantiating evidence from other areas of knowledge is always necessary. Similarly the good newspaperman does not base his views only on those expressed by people he has spoken to, but also on information available from economics, political science, and history.

As a rule, generalizations based on sampling and on the frequency of similar occurrences in the past should be used very cautiously. Only a man who has superhuman knowledge—such as Hitler, Stalin, and others like them claim to have had—is capable of asserting generalizations that purport to be completely certain. The rest of us, who are merely human, must be satisfied with severely restricted enumerative generalizations.

EXERCISES

(a) *Which of the following generalizations are definitory? Explain.*

(1) Stenography is the use of shorthand in dictation.
(2) The stenographer is usually a good typist.
(3) Triangles have three sides.
(4) The mountain lion is North American.
(5) This poem is the essence of Tennyson.
(6) Confederate money is a form of currency.
(7) As to the Adjective: when in doubt, strike it out. (Samuel Clemens.)
(8) A thing of beauty is a joy forever. (Keats.)
(9) Charm, like the fragrance of some wondrous wine,
    All can enjoy yet none can now define. (H. T. Peck.)
(10) *Jargon* is talk that is considered both ugly-sounding and hard to understand. (H. W. Fowler.)

(b) *Classify each of the following generalizations under one of the following heads:*

(*a*) *Emotive*	(*d*) *Definitory*
(*b*) *Subjective*	(*e*) *Enumerative*
(*c*) *Popular*	(*f*) *Statistical*

Discuss the reliability of each generalization.

(1) People take England on trust, and repeat that Shakespeare is the greatest of all authors; I have read him; there is nothing that compares with Racine or Corneille: his plays are unreadable, pitiful. (Napoleon.)

(2) Cancer in mice is hereditary. This was proved in postmortems made on more than 40,000 mice. It was shown that in some families cancer developed in every mouse living over eighteen months. In others, kept under identical conditions, cancer did not develop in a single member of the family.

(3) John Smith prepared himself for death: he had just read insurance statistics on life expectancy, and his time was up.

(4) According to the "Better Vision Institute" (1941) the fact that "sight is the most important sense in driving automobiles" is proved by the following statistics. Of 600 deaf-mutes permitted to drive in Pennsylvania only one was involved in an accident over a two-year period. This accident resulted from the deaf-mute's car being hit by a normal driver. During the same period 1 out of 25 automobile drivers were involved in accidents.

(5) Scarcely a day goes by without the newspaper containing an account of some paroled convict committing a crime. The bright boys have a lot of new names for it. But I say once a criminal always a criminal.

(6) Tyndall determined that putrefaction of organic matter is due to floating particles in the atmosphere. He placed 27 open sterilized flasks containing organic matter in pure mountain air. Not one indication of putrefaction was found. He placed a similar number, opened, in a hayloft. After three days only two remained clear of putrefaction.

(7) I have always suffered from hangovers when I have done a little drinking at parties. I decided to find out the *real* cause. I experimented. Monday night I had rum and soda. Result, hangover. Tuesday: rye and soda. Result, hangover. Wednesday: brandy and soda. Same result. Thursday: bourbon and

soda. Same result. Friday, Scotch and soda. Hangover. Saturday, gin and soda. Hangover. I've just got to stop drinking soda.

(8) An impartial poll proved that 90 per cent of Americans favored the repeal of the amusement tax. In order to get an unprejudiced sampling the poll-takers distributed their question-naire to *everyone* attending professional ball games during the month of July.

(9) A great famine began in Ireland in 1845, reaching its climax in 1848. Agrarian crimes showed a sharp increase during the same period, until in 1848 there were three times as many agrarian crimes as in 1845. With the return of better crops after 1848 the agrarian crime rate declined. In 1851 it was only 50 per cent higher than it was in 1845. Famine and agrarian crime are closely, probably causally, linked.

(10) Pasteur claimed the discovery of a successful anthrax vaccine on the basis of the following experiment. He inoculated 24 sheep, 1 goat, and 5 cows. He then added an equal number of animals to the herd in these proportions. He then infected all 60 animals with anthrax microbes. In two days each of the unprotected animals was either dead or dying. The vaccinated animals showed no ill effects.

HYPOTHETICAL GENERALIZATIONS, OR HYPOTHESES

Enumerative generalization is an important instrument in the attainment of reliable information. But an even more important kind of scientific generalization is *hypothesis*. Very often we are not concerned simply with the question of whether what we say of *some* can be said of *all*. Sometimes we look for causal explanations. A given phenomenon occurs and we ask: Why did this occur? In answering such a question we posit what we call *hypotheses*, causal statements which in conjunction with some fact or set of facts show why the phenomenon in question had to occur. For example, let us imagine the following amazing situation. For several weeks students in a certain course have been falling asleep during lectures. The problem is: Why? What is the answer we are looking for? It is some general principle which, once discovered, will enable us to explain what has happened. Thus to explain the sleeping students we might argue hypothetically: a) The effect to be explained: students fall asleep at lectures in a certain room. b) Possibly significant fact: the room is hot and humid. c) Hypothesis: since heat and humidity cause sleepiness, the presence of these factors in the room causes the students to sleep.

Notice that this argument is similar in form to a syllogism. In fact to formulate a hypothesis we search for some premise from which the known conclusion is logically deducible. However, there are many premises from which a phenomenon can be logically deduced. But the premises that are sought for are those that are verifiable. Thus, even though the explanation concerning the sleeping students may be logically valid, we might doubt whether a hot and humid room necessarily causes people to fall asleep. Indeed there are many hot and humid rooms in which students do *not* fall asleep. Furthermore, even if hot and humid rooms tend to put students to sleep, other causes of slumber exist and may afford a more reasonable explanation. Perhaps the lecturer is intolerably boring or has a hypnotic voice; either one of these facts might explain the slumber of his students. In any event, a good hypothesis establishes some general causal relationship which, when tested, serves to explain the event under investigation.

The discovery of a good hypothesis is usually difficult. If students fall asleep in a class, several possible explanations are available. Some very obvious facts in a student's own experience may provide a ready explanation for his particular reaction. But usually the cause is far from obvious. When Goldberger was investigating the causes of pellagra, he first entertained the hypothesis that it was caused by germs. But when he saw that neither doctors, orderlies, nor nurses caught the disease, he discounted the theory of the germs. Only after testing several hypotheses and finding them deficient did he finally accept the hypothesis that pellagra is due to a diet deficiency. Obviously if good hypotheses were easily attainable, we would know by now the causes of cancer, war, and the high cost of living.

But even when hypotheses seem to offer the best explanation, they must be verified constantly. New information is always being discovered which may cause a hypothesis to be rejected or modified. If it were found that a man had pellagra, even though he had no observable diet deficiency, important modifications in Goldberger's explanation would have to be made. Einstein made modifications of Newton's hypothesis because it could not explain newly discovered phenomena of motion at microscopic and macroscopic levels. Thus, all hypotheses are merely probable. Additional facts may always prove them wrong.

Oddly enough, false hypotheses have sometimes led to important discoveries. The Babylonians believed that there were only seven heavenly bodies, and their attempt to confirm this wrong belief led them to look for and find the planet Mercury. But false hypotheses remain false, no matter how much they may stimulate inquiry. Alchemy may have stimulated an inquiry into chemistry, but alchemy is nonetheless false.

Even though the discovery of satisfactory hypotheses is difficult, and even though they are never entirely foolproof, there are some rules which can be set down for deciding whether a sudden "brilliant" idea is a satisfactory hypothesis or merely an unwarranted guess. Knowledge of these rules will not tell us how to create hypotheses, but they will tell us what conditions must be satisfied if a hypothesis is to be given serious consideration.

1. *The first condition of a satisfactory hypothesis is that it should account for the phenomenon under investigation.* What this means is that the hypothesis must be one that really explains the facts. Thus, if we maintain that oxygen reacts to hydrogen because the former has an affinity to the latter, we are not really explaining anything. The hypothesis that something has an "affinity" for something else leaves us as much in the dark as ever. We would still have to know what the nature of this "affinity" is. Actually, such a hypothesis merely repeats the facts. It merely states that oxygen reacts with hydrogen because—oxygen reacts with hydrogen.

Similarly to explain why a war broke out by saying "conditions were ripe for it" is not really to explain anything at all. We are simply saying the war broke out because it broke out; the ripeness of conditions *meant* the war broke out. But no real explanation is given of what conditions necessitated the war.

Many theories that sound like good hypotheses have been accepted even though they contain ambiguous phrases such as "conditions are ripe." Marxists use this phrase to avoid real verification. Every time one of their predictions fails they are always able to say "conditions were *not* ripe." As a result their theories can *never* be proved false, and, as we have already seen, a doctrine that by its very formulation is incapable of ever being tested for falsehood is not a genuine hypothesis. In fact, recent events afford ample evidence of how Soviet doctrines operate on the false principle that if there is a conflict between fact and hypothesis, the fact must be changed. Thus when Beria, a very important Soviet official, was "liquidated," the very fact of his existence was eradicated. All libraries which owned the *Large Soviet Encyclopedia* were instructed to replace pages containing the picture and full biography of Beria with new pages which made no mention of him. Thus governmental theories required that the facts be made to fit the hypothesis of Marxist infallibility. In contrast, the scientist is prepared to change hypotheses of very long standing when faced with additional evidence.

In a similar fashion, hypotheses accounting for crimes must fit the facts. A detective solving a murder is creating a hypothesis. Suppose he finds a man shot through the head. The deceased has a gun in his hand, and a suicide note is lying on the desk before him. The obvious explanation is that the man shot himself. But the medical examiner discovers that the bullet has entered the skull at such an angle so as to rule out the theory of a self-inflicted wound. The theory of suicide will not account for this phenomenon. The detective must discard it and in its place substitute the conjecture of murder by person or persons unknown.

2. *A second important condition for a hypothesis is that it should be verifiable.* We should be able to make a prediction which can be tested. Any hypothesis that cannot be tested must

be viewed with suspicion. Einstein's theory was not accepted until it was subjected to searching tests, and it will be rejected if tests are devised which invalidate it.

It should be noted further that a hypothesis must specify some given space-time restrictions on the occurrence of a given event. A hypothesis that merely predicts that some event "will happen at some time in the future," without specifying the time or place, is incapable of ever being tested so that its effectiveness is nullified.

Verifiability is also an important factor employed in criminal investigations. The detective seeks to 1) find some person or persons who may have committed the crime, and 2) prove that the person or persons were at some *particular* place at some *particular* time. His hypothesis may begin with a general formula: the person who was at place "P" at time "T" probably committed the murder. He may then find evidence that Mr. X was at place "P" at time "T." He will then conclude that Mr. X probably committed the murder. Of course Mr. X might object that he did not commit the murder despite his presence at place "P." He might even point to others who were at "P" at time "T." This new information would then force the detective to revise his original view: The person who was at place "P" at time "T" and "had a motive" committed the murder. In this way criminal hypotheses constantly undergo revision as they are falsified or verified. But it is always important to remember that no verification ever makes them absolutely certain. Mr. X could have been at "P" at time "T" and "have had a motive" and yet he might not have been guilty. But the probability of his guilt increases as more and more facts connecting him with the crime are uncovered, as these newly revised hypotheses are verified, and as other possible causes are eliminated.

3. *An acceptable hypothesis should be compatible with previous well-established hypotheses.* When Leverrier maintained that there was another unknown planet beyond Uranus, his theory was in accord with the most accepted astronomical theories. However, a hypothesis can contradict previous

ones and prove to be satisfactory. Einstein's theory of relativity did contradict a number of conceptions in Newton's physics. But a contradictory hypothesis is utilized only if it is the sole alternative for explaining a phenomenon.

Similarly, hypotheses in criminal investigations never operate in a vacuum. Our fictitious Mr. X in the above example may have been at "P" at time "T" and "have had a motive." But the knowledge that Mr. X is a highly respected citizen would be important in the evaluation of the reliability of the hypothesis. Mr. X might still be guilty, but his respectability plus the possible fact that he can show other good reasons for being at "P" at time "T" must be considered in evaluating Mr. X's guilt. Of course, if Mr. X is a known criminal then the hypothesis that he is the murderer is compatible with known information. Such compatibility tends to confirm the judgment that he is guilty.

4. *Finally we should accept the hypothesis that makes the least number of assumptions.* No problem exists if one and only one hypothesis accounts for the events. But where two or more explanations exist, that one is acceptable which requires the fewest assumptions, i.e., the acceptable hypothesis should be the simplest of all those proposed. Both the Ptolemaic and the Copernican hypotheses were able to explain all the known astronomical data. The Ptolemaic belief that the sun circled the earth was just as plausible as the Copernican belief that the earth circled the sun. Both required the notion of "epicycles" to account for the motion of the heavenly bodies. But the Copernican theory required fewer such epicycles and the mathematics it employed was less complicated. Copernicus's hypothesis was the simpler of the two. This criterion, among others, made it acceptable.

This criterion also plays a role in criminal investigation. Mr. X, Mr. Y, and Mr. Z were at the scene of the crime at time "T." All had motives. All were unable to provide alibis. Who is guilty? What very often happens is that a renewed search is begun for some factor which will eliminate two of the three suspects. Also the assumptions implicit in considering Mr. X or Mr. Y or Mr. Z guilty must be made explicit. Mr. X could be guilty. But is it legitimate to *assume* that a man of his wealth and respectability would have committed the murder no matter how much he hated the victim? Further, can we *assume* that a short, fat man like Mr. X would have been able to overpower the victim as the murderer would have had to do? To both of these questions the answer can be "yes." Rich and respectable men have been known to commit murders. Short and fat men can also be very strong men. But such assumptions are very difficult to verify. For this reason the police believe that a man's guilt should be ascertained by a minimum of assumptions and a maximum of proven facts.

Recognizing the difficulty in constructing a satisfactory generalization or hypothesis, we ought to be forewarned against too ready acceptance of sweeping statements. No one ought to treat lightly the search for reliability. It is the never-ending task of all of us. Business, politics, school, and family life challenge us to look for reliable information with which we may act sensibly.

EXERCISES

(a) *Why were the following hypotheses considered satisfactory at one time, but are not so considered any longer:*

(1) Maggots and similar forms of life are produced by spontaneous generation.

(2) The rise and fall of the Nile are due to the action of the sun on water.

(3) Hydrogen combines with oxygen because hydrogen has an affinity for oxygen.

(4) Man has language because he has the faculty of speech.

(5) Mothers love their children because of the maternal instinct.

(6) An insane person is possessed by an evil spirit.

(b) *Pick out and evaluate hypotheses in each of the following, employing the four tests for determining a reliable hypothesis:*

(1) The Greek doctor Galen was examining a feverish woman patient. As he was taking her pulse, someone entered, saying he had just come from the theater where Pylades was dancing. Galen noticed an immediate quickening of the patient's pulse at the mention of the name. Next day, Galen purposely arranged that someone should enter while he was taking her pulse and say that he had just seen Morphus dancing. This and a similar test the following day produced no indications of a quickened pulse. When, however, on the fourth day, Pylades's name was again mentioned, the pulse rate jumped markedly. Galen diagnosed his patient's illness as *hereos*, love-sickness.

(2) Eristratus observed that the arteries of a live animal spout blood, but that the arteries of dead animals when dissected are found to be empty. He claimed that arteries are normally filled with air. When the arteries are cut, the air escapes, creating a vacuum which pulls blood from the veins. This blood spouts out because it is following the escaping air.

(3) When the mouth is opened wide and breath is blown upon the hand, the vapor appears to be warm. When the lips are pursed, the thin stream of vapor appears to be cold. Anaximines, who first tried the experiment, explained this phenomenon as due to the fact that rarefaction is accompanied by heat, condensation by cold.

(4) Empedocles experimented with a hollow cylinder, open at one end, almost closed at the other by a cone with only a tiny aperture. He dipped the empty cylinder in water, holding his finger over the small hole. No water entered. He then filled the cylinder with water, holding it upside-down, with his finger closing the cone. No water escaped. He argued that this was to be explained by the pressure of air.

(5) We have long observed that every neurosis has the result, and therefore probably the purpose, of forcing the patient out of real life, of alienating him from actuality. The neurotic

turns away from reality because he finds it unbearable—either the whole or part of it. (Sigmund Freud.)

(6) But at that time I overlooked one problem of great importance; and it is astonishing to me except on the principle of Columbus and his egg, how I could have overlooked it and its solution. This problem is the tendency in organic beings descended from the same stock to diverge in character as they become modified. That they have diverged greatly is obvious from the manner in which species of all kinds can be classed under genera, genera under families, families under sub-orders, and so forth. The solution as I believe, is that the modified offspring of all dominant and increasing forms tend to become adapted to many and highly diversified places in the economy of nature. (Charles Darwin.)

(7) Karl Frisch has shown that bees respond to color. He used pieces of paper in a series of 15 colors. For a time food was placed on a blue card. Then the blue cards, placed haphazardly among the shades of gray, were put down without food. In every case, the bees went at once to the blue cards.

   (c) *What hypothesis provides the best answer for each of the following:*

(1) Students who suffer from allergies generally rate 5 to 10 per cent higher in intelligence tests than non-allergic students.

(2) There are more automobile accidents at dusk than at any other time.

(3) A group of highly educated persons, given a standard sixth-grade test, fell well below the average of the sixth-grade class that had taken the same test.

(4) A patient with a dangerous tumor can be treated by a sufficient concentration of Xrays. However, the same Xray beam which is powerful enough to destroy the tumor would also destroy all the body tissue between the beam and the tumor. A weaker beam would be insufficient to destroy the tumor. How was the tumor actually destroyed with the Xray?

(5) Generally large cities in the United States tend to go Democratic while rural areas go Republican.

(6) It is curious that the Mayas in Central America developed a very high civilization in a climate that was hot and teeming with malaria. Yet some miles away there was a people living in climatic conditions that were extremely satisfactory. The culture of the latter people was almost primitive compared to the Mayan civilization.

7) Mono Lake (Nevada) is a hundred miles in a straight line from the ocean—and between it and the ocean—are one or two ranges of mountains—yet thousands of sea-gulls go there every season to lay their eggs and rear their young . . . In speaking of the peculiarities of Mono Lake, I ought to have mentioned that at intervals all around its shore stand picturesque turret-looking masses and clusters of a whitish, coarse-grained rock that resembles inferior mortar dried hard; and if one breaks off fragments of this rock he will find perfectly shaped and thoroughly petrified gulls' eggs deeply imbedded in the mass. How did they get there? I simply state the fact—for it is a fact—and leave the geological reader to crack the nut at his leisure and solve the problem after his own fashion. (Samuel Clemens.)

GENERAL EXERCISES

1. *Assume that each of the following statements is presented as reliable. How would you go about showing that they are not?*

(a) Hot weather causes dysentery.

(b) The high price of coffee is the natural result of the law of supply and demand.

(c) A man 5 feet 10 inches tall should weigh 175 pounds.

(d) "Sea Foam" is the best detergent; it gives more thick, creamy suds than any other.

(e) It would be most unusual to deal four aces in succession from a well-shuffled deck of cards.

(f) The best measure of the effectiveness of a teacher is the average of student answers to a prepared questionnaire.

(g) The music of Wagner is more beautiful than that of Brahms.

(h) Some sort or other of totalitarianism is inevitable.

(i) Political institutions are a superstructure resting upon an economic foundation.

(j) Before embarking upon the solution of "problems" some effort should be made by the trustees of foundations to make certain that their solution is in the public interest.

---

2. *The following selection gives first Poe's poem, "The Raven," and then part of his account of how he wrote it. Read both poem and explanation; then answer the questions at the end.*

THE RAVEN

Once upon a midnight dreary, while I pondered, weak and weary,
Over many a quaint and curious volume of forgotten lore—
While I nodded, nearly napping, suddenly there came a tapping,
As of some one gently rapping, rapping at my chamber door.
" 'Tis some visitor," I muttered, "tapping at my chamber door—
                    Only this and nothing more."

Ah, distinctly I remember, it was in the bleak December;
And each separate dying ember wrought its ghost upon the floor.
Eagerly I wished the morrow;—vainly I had sought to borrow
From my books surcease of sorrow—sorrow for the lost Lenore—
For the rare and radiant maiden whom the angels name Lenore—
                    Nameless *here* for evermore.

And the silken, sad, uncertain rustling of each purple curtain
Thrilled me—filled me with fantastic terrors never felt before;
So that now, to still the beating of my heart I stood repeating
" 'Tis some visitor entreating entrance at my chamber door—
Some late visitor entreating entrance at my chamber door;—
                    This it is and nothing more."

Presently my soul grew stronger; hesitating then no longer,
"Sir," said I, "or Madam, truly your forgiveness I implore;
But the fact is I was napping, and so gently you came rapping,
And so faintly you came tapping, tapping at my chamber door,
That I scarce was sure I heard you"—here I opened wide the door;—
    Darkness there and nothing more.

Deep into that darkness peering, long I stood there wondering,
 fearing,
Doubting, dreaming dreams no mortal ever dared to dream before;
But the silence was unbroken, and the stillness gave no token,
And the only word there spoken was the whispered word, "Lenore!"
This I whispered, and an echo murmured back the word "Lenore!"
    Merely this and nothing more.

Back into the chamber turning, all my soul within me burning,
Soon again I heard a tapping somewhat louder than before.
"Surely," said I, "surely that is something at my window lattice;
Let me see, then, what thereat is, and this mystery explore—
Let my heart be still a moment and this mystery explore;—
    'Tis the wind and nothing more!"

Open here I flung the shutter, when, with many a flirt and flutter
In there stepped a stately Raven of the saintly days of yore.
Not the least obeisance made he; not a minute stopped or stayed he;
But, with mien of lord or lady, perched above my chamber door—
Perched upon a bust of Pallas just above my chamber door—
    Perched, and sat, and nothing more.

Then this ebony bird beguiling my sad fancy into smiling,
By the grave and stern decorum of the countenance it wore,
"Though thy crest be shorn and shaven, thou," I said, "art sure
 no craven,
Ghastly grim and ancient Raven wandering from the Nightly shore—
Tell me what thy lordly name is on the Night's Plutonian shore!"
    Quoth the Raven, "Nevermore."

Much I marvelled this ungainly fowl to hear discourse so plainly,
Though its answer little meaning—little relevancy bore;

For we cannot help agreeing that no living human being
Ever yet was blessed with seeing bird above his chamber door—
Bird or beast upon the sculptured bust above his chamber door,
                    With such name as "Nevermore."

But the Raven, sitting lonely on the placid bust, spoke only
That one word, as if his soul in that one word he did outpour.
Nothing farther then he uttered—not a feather then he fluttered—
Till I scarcely more than muttered "Other friends have flown
    before—
On the morrow *he* will leave me, as my hopes have flown before."
                    Then the bird said, "Nevermore."

Startled at the stillness broken by reply so aptly spoken,
"Doubtless," said I, "what it utters is its only stock and store
Caught from some unhappy master whom unmerciful Disaster
Followed fast and followed faster till his songs one burden bore—
Till the dirges of his Hope that melancholy burden bore
                    Of 'Never—nevermore.'"

But the Raven still beguiling all my fancy into smiling,
Straight I wheeled a cushioned seat in front of bird, and bust and
    door;
Then, upon the velvet sinking, I betook myself to linking
Fancy unto fancy, thinking what this ominous bird of yore—
What this grim, ungainly, ghastly, gaunt, and ominous bird of yore
                    Meant in croaking "Nevermore."

This I sat engaged in guessing, but no syllable expressing
To the fowl whose fiery eyes now burned into my bosom's core;
This and more I sat divining, with my head at ease reclining
On the cushion's velvet lining that the lamplight gloated o'er,
But whose velvet violet lining with the lamplight gloating o'er,
                    She shall press, ah, nevermore!

Then, methought, the air grew denser, perfumed from an unseen
    censer
Swung by Seraphim whose foot-falls tinkled on the tufted floor.

"Wretch," I cried, "thy God hath lent thee—by these angels he
    hath sent thee
Respite—respite and nepenthe from thy memories of Lenore;
Quaff, oh, quaff this kind nepenthe, and forget this lost Lenore!"
                            Quoth the Raven, "Nevermore."

"Prophet!" said I, "thing of evil! prophet still, if bird or
    devil!—
Whether Tempter sent, or whether tempest tossed thee here ashore,
Desolate yet all undaunted, on this desert land enchanted—
On this home by Horror haunted—tell me truly, I implore—
Is there—*is* there balm in Gilead?—tell me—tell me, I implore!"
                            Quoth the Raven, "Nevermore."

"Prophet!" said I, "thing of evil! prophet still, if bird or
    devil!
By that Heaven that bends above us—by that God we both adore—
Tell this soul with sorrow laden if, within the distant Aidenn,
It shall clasp a sainted maiden whom the angels name Lenore—
Clasp a rare and radiant maiden whom the angels name Lenore."
                            Quoth the Raven, "Nevermore."

"Be that word our sign of parting, bird or fiend!" I shrieked,
    upstarting—
"Get thee back into the tempest and the Night's Plutonian shore!
Leave no black plume as a token of that lie thy soul hath spoken!
Leave my loneliness unbroken!—quit the bust above my door!
Take thy beak from out my heart, and take thy form from off my
    door!"
                            Quoth the Raven, "Nevermore."

And the Raven, never flitting, still is sitting, *still* is sitting
On the pallid bust of Pallas just above my chamber door;
And his eyes have all the seeming of a demon's that is dreaming,
And the lamp-light o'er him streaming throws his shadow on the
    floor;
And my soul from out that shadow that lies floating on the floor
                        Shall be lifted—nevermore!

A portion of Poe's explanation of how he wrote "The Raven,"
from his "The Philosophy of Composition," follows:

Let us dismiss, as irrelevant to the poem, *per se*, the circum-
stance—or say the necessity—which, in the first place, gave
rise to the intention of composing *a* poem that should suit at
once the popular and the critical taste.

We commence, then, with this intention.

The initial consideration was that of extent. If any literary
work is too long to be read at one sitting, we must be content
to dispense with the immensely important effect derivable from
unity of impression—for, if two sittings be required, the affairs
of the world interfere, and every thing like totality is at once
destroyed. But since, *ceteris paribus*, no poet can afford to dispense with *any thing* that may advance his design, it but remains to be seen whether there is, in extent, any advantage to
counterbalance the loss of unity which attends it. Here I say
no, at once. What we term a long poem, is, in fact, merely a
succession of brief ones—that is to say, of brief poetical effects.
It is needless to demonstrate that a poem is such, only inasmuch
as it intensely excites, by elevating, the soul; and all intense
excitements are, through a psychal necessity, brief. For this
reason, at least one half of the "Paradise Lost" is essentially
prose—a succession of poetical excitements interspersed, *inevitably*, with corresponding depressions—the whole being deprived,
through the extremeness of its length, of the vastly important
artistic element, totality, or unity, of effect.

It appears evident, then, that there is a distinct limit, as
regards length, to all works of literary art—the limit of a single
sitting—and that, although in certain classes of prose composition, such as "Robinson Crusoe," (demanding no unity,) this
limit may be advantageously overpassed, it can never properly
be overpassed in a poem. Within this limit, the extent of a
poem may be made to bear mathematical relation to its merit—
in other words, to the excitement or elevation—again, in other
words, to the degree of the true poetical effect which it is
capable of inducing; for it is clear that the brevity must be in
direct ratio of the intensity of the intended effect:—this, with

one proviso—that a certain degree of duration is absolutely requisite for the production of any effect at all.

Holding in view these considerations, as well as that degree of excitement which I deemed not above the popular, while not below the critical, taste, I reached at once what I conceived the proper *length* for my intended poem—a length of about one hundred lines. It is, in fact, a hundred and eight.

My next thought concerned the choice of an impression, or effect, to be conveyed: and here I may as well observe that, throughout the construction, I kept steadily in view the design of rendering the work *universally* appreciable. I should be carried too far out of my immediate topic were I to demonstrate a point upon which I have repeatedly insisted, and which, with the poetical, stands not in the slightest need of demonstration —the point, I mean, that Beauty is the sole legitimate province of the poem. A few words, however, in elucidation of my real meaning, which some of my friends have evinced a disposition to misrepresent. That pleasure which is at once the most intense, the most elevating, and the most pure, is, I believe, found in the contemplation of the beautiful. When, indeed, men speak of Beauty, they mean, precisely, not a quality, as is supposed, but an effect—they refer, in short, just to that intense and pure elevation of *soul*—*not* of intellect, or of heart— upon which I have commented, and which is experienced in consequence of contemplating "the beautiful." Now I designate Beauty as the province of the poem, merely because it is an obvious rule of Art that effect should be made to spring from direct causes—that objects should be attained through means best adapted for their attainment—no one as yet having been weak enough to deny that the peculiar elevation alluded to is *most readily* attained in the poem. Now the object, Truth, or the satisfaction of the intellect, and the object Passion, or the excitement of the heart, are, although attainable, to a certain extent, in poetry, far more readily attainable in prose. Truth, in fact, demands a precision, and Passion a *homeliness* (the truly passionate will comprehend me) which are absolutely antagonistic to that Beauty which, I maintain, is the excitement, or pleasurable elevation, of the soul. It by no means follows from any thing here said, that passion, or even truth, may not be introduced, and even profitably introduced, into a poem—for they may serve in elucidation, or aid the general effect, as do discords in music, by contrast—but the true artist will always contrive, first, to tone them into proper subservience to the predominant aim, and, secondly, to enveil them, as far as possible, in that Beauty which is the atmosphere and the essence of the poem.

Regarding, then, Beauty, as my province, my next question referred to the *tone* of its highest manifestation—and all experience has shown that this tone is one of *sadness*. Beauty of whatever kind, in its supreme development, invariably excites the sensitive soul to tears. Melancholy is thus the most legitimate of all the poetical tones.

QUESTIONS

1) Does Dewey's analysis of the five steps of thinking fit Poe's account of his "creative" reasoning?

2) Are you satisfied that Poe's account of how he wrote the poem is reliable?

(a) Are Poe's grounds for considering *extent* to be the initial consideration in writing a poem sufficiently well established?

(b) Are his reasons for arriving at an ideal length of 100 lines satisfactory?

(c) Does he define Beauty to your satisfaction?

(d) Does Poe seek to give verification of his distinction between Beauty and Truth—Passion?

(e) How does Poe actually arrive at his statement about melancholy being the most legitimate of all poetical tones? Would you accept this statement from the evidence given?

RECOMMENDED READINGS

Lionel Ruby, *Logic*. (Philadelphia: J. B. Lippincott Co., 1950)
    Chapters 14, 15, 18.
Max Black, *Critical Thinking*, Second edition. (New York:
    Prentice-Hall, 1952) Chapters 13–19.
Irving Copi, *Introduction to Logic*. (New York: The Macmillan
    Co.) Chapters 13, 14.
Morris R. Cohen and Ernest Nagel, *Logic and Scientific
    Method*. (New York: Harcourt, Brace & Co., 1934) Chap-
    ters 11, 14, 15, 16.

AVOIDING ERROR

THE difficulty with such analysis as has been undertaken in this book is that it must appear largely negative. Thinking straight seems a matter of avoiding all the temptations, glaring and subtle, to give way to emotion, to daydreaming, to believing what seems most pleasant to believe. And responsible use of language seems largely to involve avoiding the misunderstandings which arise because meanings are fluid, and because language structure is not amenable to strictly logical-mathematical procedures. It is unfortunate that no one yet has come up with a mechanical device for eliminating the gap between the frailties of human nature and reliable thinking, between the poetry of language, and the mathematical demands of pure logic. Although this book has attempted to narrow the gap, the concluding chapter can offer no palliative, panacea, or sure cure. Instead, by way of summary and review, some of the basic obstacles to obtaining and communicating reliable information will be discussed. These obstacles will be arranged, for utility and ease of reference, under three main headings: Emotional Argument, Faulty Reasoning, Misuse of Language.

EMOTIONAL ARGUMENT

Argument *ad Hominem*. When someone attempts to argue by attacking the personal character of his opponent, he is making what is called an argument *ad hominem*. For example, in a discussion on higher wages, if the proponent of higher wages is a union official, his opponent may be strongly tempted to resort to the argument *ad hominem* by pointing out that the union official's argument must be discounted because he is an "interested party," a member of the union. But knowledge of a man's motives and attitudes has no bearing on the correctness of his argument, except in so far as it causes us to be much more careful in evaluating the argument. The question of whether a man is "right" or "wrong" does not depend on his occupation or his personality.

Very often the *ad hominem* argument is very vicious. Some people characteristically argue by making personal slurs against their opponents. They will say a particular person is wrong because he is a Jew or a Catholic, a Fascist or a Communist. Because name calling is frequently as effective as it is misleading, courts of law have strict rules to govern the attempts of lawyers to discredit witnesses in cross-examination. A lawyer may criticize the personal character of a witness only if such criticism is directly connected with the reliability of evidence. Thus the state of a man's eyesight would be highly relevant to his testimony concerning an accident he observed from a distance. But his marital status, for instance the fact that he had just married his fifth wife, would be totally irrelevant to the testimony.

A new dimension has been given to the *ad hominem* argument in recent years through the popularization of discoveries in psychology. Now if a man argues for social security he is told that he argues this way because he has an "inferiority complex," or if he argues too strongly for free enterprise he has a "superiority complex." But it should be apparent that one does not answer an argument merely by pointing out that an individual has a "complex" of some kind. A scientist may have neurotic tendencies and may beat his wife, but these facts do not discredit his theories.

Genetic Fallacy.   This fallacy involves the attempt to destroy the value of an argument by criticising its origin. Thus, some have argued that religion is no more than a superstition because it originated out of superstition. But even if it is true that religious views resulted from superstition, this does not mean that such views are still to be equated with superstition. Even though chemistry originated in alchemy, chemistry is not therefore to be regarded as a prejudiced and superstitious study. Yet the appeal to "bad" origin is often sufficient to arouse enough emotion so that the real argument is obliterated.

The attempt to discredit an argument by reflecting on the proponent's background combines the *genetic fallacy* with the *ad hominem*. But because a man has grown up in a bad family and a worse environment, it does not follow that he himself is a bad human being nor does it follow that his arguments are false. Conversely a man who comes from a good family and a good environment does not always turn out to be a good human being.

In a more subtle way some social scientists have fallen into this fallacy by claiming that human beings are merely products of their environment. But a man may come from a very bad environment and still grow up to be a normal, healthy human being.

Appeal to the People.   Because the public speaker or writer must gain the confidence of his audience if he is to make his point, he may often attempt to establish an atmosphere of friendliness. One of the ways in which he accomplishes this is by depicting himself as "one of the boys." The use of such expressions as "fellow citizens" or "friends and neighbors" is primarily an attempt to make an audience friendly and responsive. A similar purpose is served by such statements as "We're all Americans here and we all share one great ideal, etc.," or "I'm a fellow worker. You and I know how tough it is to earn a buck. My talk ain't fancy, but . . ." or "Because I am addressing a college-trained audience, I know that I can speak of difficult matters seriously." Generally, such appeals are not very dangerous. But when demagogues use them to stir up strong emotions, then the consequences can be disastrous. Lynch mobs have often been formed as a result of strong emotional appeal to group unity.

In its more subtle forms the appeal to the people occurs when we try to meet an argument by saying "it isn't natural" or "it isn't common sense." People once used to argue that flying machines were "not natural" and "against common sense." But such criticisms are totally irrelevant to the argument.

The Appeal to Pity. The appeal to the people relies for its effect on the feeling of group unity. But a similar effect can be obtained when pity and sympathy are aroused. Lawyers will frequently use this means to defend a client. They have him wear shabby clothes, and then try to arouse the jury's sympathy by pointing out how he has suffered. Similarly, MacArthur's use of the refrain "Old soldiers never die; they just fade away" was designed to arouse sympathy and pity. In fact, anyone who argues by describing examples of personal persecution or martyrdom is appealing to pity and sympathy, rather than logic and evidence.

Appeals to the people and to pity can be important rhetorical devices, for in these ways effective speakers are able to arouse desired emotions. Unfortunately, effective speakers are not always effective thinkers, and only too often people have been led by demagogues who were effective persuaders but bad reasoners. Some congressmen have succeeded in getting their audience to weep with them and for them. They arouse reactions, not thought. But the *method of persuasion* and the *method of reasoning* must always be clearly differentiated.

The Appeal to Authority. This fallacy arises when we attempt to justify an idea by appealing to authority. Thus for many years people refused to accept the theory of evolution because it seemed to contradict the Bible and the Church Fathers. But the truth or falsity of a doctrine rests on the empirical and logical evidence that is given for it. Even the most scientifically attested hypothesis is not made acceptable merely because Einstein or some other scientist approves of it; rather it is accepted because of the empirical evidence which attests to the reliability of the hypothesis. Einstein does not make the theory of relativity true, any more than a man of distinction makes a whisky good. On the contrary, Einstein would probably have been the first to claim that the theory is not based on his *word*, but rather on the evidence which anyone could obtain if he had the proper training in mathematics and the natural sciences.

Of course there is good reason to rely on authorities, but only when their views have been carefully examined to determine (1) whether they have based these views on verifiable fact and not merely subjective feelings, and (2) whether they are *really* authorities. The fact that a scientist is an expert in physics does not automatically make him an expert in political science. Eisenhower may be a great military general, but this does not qualify him to be an expert scientist.

Appeal to Force. The attempt to gain a point by threatening physical or other harm is an *appeal to force*. The appeal to force is resorted to more subtly when it is insinuated that a person may "lose his job" or "be reported to the authorities" because of his beliefs. It also occurs when an argument is attacked as "dangerous." In such instances we try to *destroy* rather than *resolve* the argument.

An infamous example of the use of the appeal to force appears in Thucydides' account of the Athenian attempt to "persuade" the small island of Melos to join them.

"You know," says the Athenian, "as well as we do, that, in the logic of human nature, Right only comes into question where there is a balance of power, while it is Might that determines what the strong extort and the weak concede . . . Your strongest weapons are hopes yet unrealized, while the weapons in your hand are somewhat inadequate for holding out against the forces already ar-

rayed against you . . . Reflect . . . that you are taking a
decision for your country . . . a country whose fate hangs
upon a single decision right or wrong."

(Toynbee's translation.)

It is important to remember that appeals to force are rarely
this obvious. Whenever there is a hidden threat to an opponent's social, economic, or political status, the appeal to force
is being used.

FAULTY REASONING

Faulty Generalization. Any sweeping claim which is based
on a very few selected instances is a faulty generalization. A
statement such as "Foreigners just don't understand democracy"
is usually based on hearsay or on one or two unfavorable en-
counters with foreigners. A fairly common type of faulty generalization rests on the acceptance of slogans, proverbs, or
"tabloids." In the 1932 presidential election the Republicans
told the nation to keep them in office because "You shouldn't
change horses in the middle of the stream." The Democrats
answered by saying "It's time for a new deal." In 1952 the
slogans were reversed. People have often been told "never put
off for tomorrow what you can do today," that is, when not
told that "haste makes waste." Men who have associated with
Communists are often regarded suspiciously because "birds of
a feather flock together." The reply is, "You can't judge a book
by its cover." Such slogans or proverbs are clever and often persuasive. But for the important purpose of deciding whether or
not an argument is sound they are useless.

Sometimes a generalization is accepted as an unalterable
truth. An argument against wartime censorship of the press on
the basis of the statement, "Democracy can exist only as
long as the press is free," ignores the fact that all generalizations
hold only for specific circumstances and that this particular
generalization might not hold under other circumstances. Even
an important generalization such as "Thou shalt not kill"

may have exceptions; soldiers are permitted to break this rule, and so are those who kill in self-defense.

The *Post Hoc Ergo Propter Hoc* Fallacy. (After this, therefore because of this.) This fallacy occurs when the cause of some occurrence is attributed to an event that immediately preceded it, as when our stomach-ache is attributed to the last meal eaten, a causal relationship which might or might not be true. Sequence of events does not necessarily imply causal relationship. Yet people constantly think that, because event X occurred immediately before event Y, therefore event X is the *cause* of event Y. "I walked under a ladder; I failed the exam I had immediately afterward; therefore walking under the ladder was the cause of my failure." Superstitions are generally based on the *post hoc* fallacy. Political success has frequently been based on the argument: "See! Since I've been in office, things have gone well."

Newspapers sometimes make clever use of the *post hoc* fallacy. Thus such headlines as MINERS STRIKE; REDS GAIN IN KOREA may refer to two completely independent events. But linking the two events in the same headline gives the impression to many readers that the Communists are gaining in Korea *because* the miners are striking.

If something occurred just prior to an event it is not necessarily the cause of the event. An infinite number of things all over the universe occur the second before a given event. One of these may be the cause. But much more knowledge is required than the simple fact that it occurred a second or even a split second before the happening.

Begging the Question—Circular Reasoning. Begging the question, or reasoning in circular fashion, consists in the mere reassertion of the meaning of the premises in the conclusion. In its most obvious form it can be seen in the argument: "John is a good man. Why? Because he's good, that's why." In this example the conclusion "John is a good man" does no more than repeat the premise.

Of course begging the question is usually not this obvious.

Usually the premise is repeated but in different words: "John is a good man. Why? Because he is virtuous." But it should be apparent that "virtuous" and "good" are synonymous and therefore the argument is circular.

Sometimes an argument is quite complex and then it is more difficult to check for circularity: "Freud claims that we are often frustrated because our sex drives are blocked and they become blocked because we are thwarted in our desires." The circularity here may be difficult to discover until "frustrated" is seen to have the same meaning as "thwarted in our desires."

Special Pleading. This fallacy occurs when a deliberate attempt is made to "stack the cards" in favor of some given position. Politicians are notoriously adept in employing this fallacy. They very often completely ignore or refuse to look for any evidence that could invalidate their views. In the fourth chapter—the chapter on logic—the student's theme on the United Nations was criticized as unreliable. What the instructor meant was that the student was engaged in "special pleading." He had completely ignored any evidence that might show the United Nations in a favorable light despite the fact that many important people have defended the United Nations.

In a sense all of us are engaged in "special pleading." When we favor some position we tend to minimize any data that criticize the position. Lawyers are often concerned with *minimizing* unfavorable evidence. But only a dishonest lawyer would deliberately *ignore* such evidence.

The Appeal to Ignorance. This fallacy consists in an attempt to justify a belief even if there is no evidence for it. Thus people will sometimes be found to argue: "The occurrence of psychic phenomena is indeed a fact because no one has ever disproved it." But because something has never been proved *false*, it is not therefore to be considered true. The statement "A green-eyed elf sits on the other side of the moon" may not ever be disproved. But this does not mean that an elf does sit on the other side of the moon.

Irrelevance. This fallacy is probably the most frequently used. We start out by trying to prove one statement and then end up by trying to prove a different statement. Women sometimes argue in the following way:

Mrs. X: But she's so stupid! Every time you ask her a question she has nothing to say. Furthermore, I know her I.Q. is very low.

Mrs. Y: But wasn't that a nice blouse she was wearing?

In this example Mrs. X is trying to prove someone's stupidity. But Mrs. Y diverts the issue into another channel.

Examples abound in English themes, as in the following excerpt from a theme:

In this paper I should like to comment on Ibsen's *Ghosts*. The play was very sincere and honest. Sincerity and honesty are two qualities that are very praiseworthy. All people should be sincere and honest.

The student begins the theme by telling us he will discuss Ibsen's *Ghosts*. But he concludes by telling us that sincerity and honesty are good qualities.

Imperfect Analogy. Analogy is frequently a very compelling method of reasoning. For example, we might argue: "Conditions today are like conditions prior to World War II. Therefore, since war followed then, war will follow now." Similarly, Spengler argued that since conditions in modern Western civilization are just like those which were present during the decline of many ancient civilizations, Western civilization is also in the process of declining. But analogies of this kind can be satisfactory only if they compare two elements that have very few differences. We can argue that one tomato will be like all the others because one tomato is not different in any important respects from another, that is, tomatoes are generally considered to be homogeneous. But analogy is of little value in comparing civilizations. There are just as many important differences among civilizations as there are similarities.

When we ignore differences and base analogy on a few similarities, we are involved in the fallacy of imperfect analogy.

Unfortunately, analogy has found frequent use as a dangerous political weapon. At one time it was fashionable to argue that circular motion was natural because the earth revolved around the sun. Consequently, it was also natural for society to consist of a monarch around whom the rest of the nation revolved. Marxists have frequently argued that opposition of social classes is necessary in capitalistic societies by analogy with the opposition of physical forces in the universe.

However, analogy can sometimes serve a useful purpose in suggesting new and fruitful approaches to problems. The study of animal behavior has led to important clues concerning the principles motivating human behavior. The analogy between the flow of electricity through a wire and the flow of water through a tube served to stimulate the search for new and more complex properties of electricity. But such advantages of analogy must be weighed against the disadvantages.

MISUSE OF LANGUAGE

Misuse of Metaphor. The argument from analogy rests on presumed resemblances between otherwise unrelated events. Similar to analogy is *metaphor*, the use of a word to express a likeness. But whereas analogy usually rests upon a number of resemblances, metaphor utilizes only a limited number of resemblances. People are called "tigers," "angels," "wolves," "monsters," and so forth on the basis of one or two characteristics. Such metaphors are sometimes picturesque, sometimes clever, but very often they are misleading and confusing. They cause us to oversimplify our judgments of people and to attribute too much or too little to them. Calling a man a "tiger," for example, causes us to attribute to him many characteristics which he may not really possess—anger, hatred, ferocity, etc. Mark Twain's novel, *Pudd'nhead Wilson*, provides a good illustration. On the basis of one remark, Wilson, a promising young lawyer, new to a small town, was called "pudd'nhead."

It took years for him to establish his practice because the townspeople judged him by the name he was given.

Metaphor, like analogy, is faulty only when it is misused, as it is in the following:

> Tree planting and similar *soft-headed quack remedies* would be in vogue. The dollar would be dishonest. The budget would be a national *laughing stock*. A spending *orgy* would be *gaining a momentum* which could hardly be checked. Class prejudice would be *rampant*. The treasury would have been *looted*.

The writer had misgivings about what would happen when Roosevelt became president of the United States in 1932, but notice that by his use of the italicized metaphors his misgivings are made to appear as if they related to actual events. Or, again, an editorial (1933) presents the following highly emotional metaphorical warning:

> Whatever menace appears to these rights is a *dread specter* before the women of America of wrecked homes, wrecked lives, and a WRECKED FUTURE.

It is somewhat of a relief to discover that the warning was occasioned by a bill before Congress which would license interstate corporations!

A very glaring example of the misuse of metaphor is seen in the following:

> [Winston Churchill], the archbishop of torydom, came to tell us how we shall live. And what is the life he maps for us? An Anglo-American tyranny to ride roughshod over the globe. He said that it was against Communism that he wanted the armies and navies combined. The words are Churchill's but the plan is Hitler's. Churchill's own domain of plunder is ripping at the seams and he asks Americans to save it for him. We are to be the trigger men, we are to provide him billions in money to regain what the robber barons are losing. (*New Masses*, March 19, 1946.)

Notice how various pictorial phrases such as "archbishop of torydom," "domain of plunder," "ripping at the seams," "trigger men," and "robber barons" are able to convey the impression that Churchill is a criminal, trying to get us to join his "gang." The writing is colorful and vivid and serves to build up in our minds an association between Churchill and the "typical gangster." And, of course, this is precisely the association that the paragraph seeks to convey. But we are duped by metaphorical writing when we accept such writing as if it were actually true.

Hypostatization. Not only may the unscrupulous writer take advantage of the normal uncritical response to metaphor, but he may also avail himself of a tendency in people to assume that abstract words refer to concrete entities. This tendency to speak of *democracy, justice, liberty,* as if they had reference to specific entities, is called *hypostatization.* The fallacy could be defined as a failure to distinguish between abstract and concrete words. The objects referred to by *table* and *chair* can be pointed to; the ideas represented by *justice* and *truth* cannot be pointed to. Examples of hypostatization can be found everywhere, as is suggested in the following list of slogans:

The State can do no wrong.
Nature decrees what is right.
The Spirit of the Nation produces its art and literature.
Science makes Progress.
Democracy safeguards human liberty.

The effect of hypostatization is—like metaphor—to produce emotion. A statement, "Justice triumphs over all," has emotional appeal. But it is too abstract to convey information about any specific situation.

Semantic Ambiguity or Equivocation. Almost all words are potentially ambiguous because almost all words have more than one meaning. Actually the meaning of a word is governed chiefly by the context in which it is found, as, for example, *bad* in the following sentences:

Susie, don't be bad.
He feels bad.
She's not a bad number.
That's too bad.
It was a bad day at Black Rock.

When deliberately or mistakenly we use the same word with different meanings in the same context we are said to "equivocate." Equivocation causes trouble because of the habitually uncritical use of language. We tend to forget that a word has many meanings, so that meaning A which Mr. X has in mind may be very different from meaning B which Mr. Y has in mind, although both are using the same word.

Mr. X: Don't you agree that *progress* is very important for a nation?
Mr. Y: Yes, I agree with you.
Several days later:
Mr. X: to a friend: Mr. Y and I are in complete agreement. We both believe in *progress*, that is, that contemporary institutions should never be allowed to deteriorate. Therefore, I'm sure he will vote against a revision of the constitution.

This example is an instance of *apparent* agreement but *real* disagreement. The following is an instance of *real* agreement but *apparent* disagreement.

Mr. X: I think you're wrong. Men are not *equal*. Some are stronger than others. Some have more intelligence.
Mr. Y: You're wrong. They are *equal*. The law states that as far as the law is concerned each man is supposed to get *equal* treatment.
Mr. X: Oh, I agree. I admit that every man is supposed to receive *equal* treatment in law courts. I thought you meant that all men have the same physical and intellectual abilities.

Equivocation can be used to make a point effectively, with no attempt at dishonesty, as with Benjamin Franklin's witty equivocation, "If we don't hang together, we'll hang separately." His equivocation served simply to enforce the grave reality behind his words. But equivocation is only too frequently used dishonestly. The communist dictatorship has developed a technique of equivocation which George Orwell has satirized in *Animal Farm*, where he imagines an animal revolution led by the pigs. When the animals have triumphed, the pigs take the place of the old human masters, and the revolution which began with the slogan "All animals are *equal*" ends with the pigs proclaiming the equivocation, "All animals are *equal*. But some animals are more *equal* than others."

Syntactic Ambiguity. Not only words, but also the *structure of sentences* (syntax) may cause confusion. Ambiguity resulting from faulty sentence structure is termed *syntactic ambiguity*. Here are a few examples:

1. Horse shows increased profits.
2. State plan aids devastated area.
3. Out of gas she had to walk home.
4. With her enormous nose aimed toward the sky my mother rushed to the plane.

A subtle form of syntactic ambiguity is called the *complex question*. This question is usually so phrased that any answer to it is self-incriminating.

Mr. Jones: Have you stopped avoiding people you owe money to?
Mr. Smith: No.
Mr. Jones: Oh, so you're still avoiding them, you rascal.
Mr. Smith: I meant "yes."
Mr. Jones: Oh, so you've been avoiding them, just as I thought.

Some lawyers employ such techniques deliberately. A witness who is asked, "When did you buy the murder weapon?" cannot answer without admitting that he owned the weapon.

Not only lawyers but politicians and editorial writers frequently employ the technique of the complex question. For example, during the Roosevelt-Truman administrations newspapers frequently made use of the complex question, "Are you going to stop this trend toward Socialism?" This was an unfair question because both the "yes" and "no" answer imply that such a trend existed. Writers of "letters to the editor" make use of the complex question, as in the following: "Are the financial resources of this government without a limit, that four billion dollars can be applied for purposes that will eventually damn the American people?" Any way this question is answered would involve damaging admissions.

Pauses and emphasis can be used to make syntactic distinctions. The sentence "America without her security is lost" can give two different meanings depending on punctuation or pauses in speech:

America, without her, security is lost.
America, without her security, is lost.

The meaning of almost any sentence is subject to alteration through emphasis. If after a dinner party someone said, "I enjoyed the dinner," he would not want to emphasize the I, "*I* enjoyed the dinner," because this might imply that the others had not. Emphasis on *dinner* might suggest that he *at least* found this part of the evening, *the dinner*, enjoyable. As he was leaving with his friends, he would not say, "*I* had a good time." Again the implication would be that the others had not enjoyed themselves. Mark Antony's funeral address in Shakespeare's *Julius Caesar* is a brilliant example of the way in which emphasis can be used to sway an audience.

EXERCISES

In what way does each of the following excerpts illustrate one or more of the errors described in this chapter?

(1) "A man must conform himself to Nature's laws, *be* verily in communion with Nature and the truth of things, or

Nature will answer him, No, not at all! . . . Nature bursts up in fireflames, French Revolutions and such like, proclaiming with terrible veracity that forged notes are forged." (Carlyle, *Heroes, Hero-worship.*)

(2) ". . . a true critic, in the perusal of a book, is like a dog at a feast, whose thoughts and stomach are wholly set upon what the guests fling away, and consequently apt to snarl most when there are the fewest bones." (Swift, A *Tale of a Tub.*)

(3) "No man ever knows, or can know, what will be the ultimate result to himself, or to others, of any given line of conduct. But every man may know, and most of us do know, what is a just and unjust act. And all of us may know also that the consequences of justice will be ultimately the best possible. . . ." (Ruskin, *Unto This Last.*)

(4) "We rely on the natural tendency of the human intellect to truth, and on the natural tendency of society to improvement . . . History is full of the signs of this natural progress of society. We see in almost every part of the annals of mankind how the industry of individuals, struggling up against wars, taxes, famines, conflagrations, mischievous prohibitions, and more mischievous protections, creates faster than government can squander, and repairs whatever invaders can destroy." (Macaulay, "Southey's Colloquies.")

(5) "Historical experience . . . shows with terrible clarity that with any mixing of the blood of the Aryan with lower races the result was the end of the culture-bearer." (Hitler, *Mein Kampf.*)

(6) "No man with a genius for legislation has appeared in America. They are rare in the history of the world. There are orators, politicians, and eloquent men, by the thousand; but the speaker has not yet opened his mouth to speak who is capable of settling the much-vexed questions of the day." (Thoreau, *Civil Disobedience.*)

(7) Is the inside of a ripe watermelon red before it is opened?

(8) The early Christians can easily be regarded as Communists.

(9) Nothing is too good for him.

(10) You will get everything you've got coming to you.

(11) Bangor *News* Moves . . . The Bangor *Daily News* is a lineal descendant of the first newspaper ever published in America.
     The entire operation required somewhat less than 24 hours. . . .

(12) In 1952 Russia asked for a Four Power Conference to "restore an independent peace-loving democratic Germany." Although this was also the professed aim of American diplomacy, no headway was made. Secretary Acheson claimed that a primary reason for the breakdown of the conference was that the Russians defined the key-words arbitrarily in the following way:
Independent: Used most frequently to describe countries with the outward trappings of sovereignty but which are actually under Soviet control.
Democratic: Used exclusively for countries or groups dominated by elements which recognize the political authority of Moscow.
Peace-loving: Applied to anything which advances the cause of the Communist parties and the authority of the Communist Party of Moscow.
On the other hand, the Russians claimed that the Americans used the terms crookedly to describe imperialistic nations like America and England.

(13) Herodotus tells how King Croesus, relying on the language of the Delphic oracle, challenged the might of the Persian king. Croesus was defeated. The oracle had said: "If Croesus attacks the Persians, he will destroy a mighty empire."

(14) Macbeth felt secure when he heard the prophecy:
   Macbeth shall never vanquish'd be until
   Great Birnam wood to high Dunsinane hill
   Shall come against him. . . .

But a forest did "come against him" when its leaves and
twigs were used to camouflage men.

(15) "Hercules the dragon will slay."

(16) Walking across the street, the Woolworth Building
came in sight.

(17) You should not major in English literature, for then
you may become an English teacher, and what kind of world
would we have if everyone was an English teacher? Who would
do the menial jobs?

*The following are excerpts from letters to the editor, edito-
rials and articles in various newspapers.*

(18) So our government is going to spend 22 million for
roads! This goes on forever—all on the cuff.
A working and honest capitalistic system has been destroyed
by the New Dealers for political advantage. Now the Dewey
Republicans are trying to outdo the New Deal.
No one denies the use of money for defense or help of the
needy, but the present wastage is almost beyond conception.
We are already socialized by taxation. If we are to be a capitalistic nation, we must have a base for money—not paper and
ink and bookkeeping.
If I steal a ham, I go to jail. But organized groups can have
laws passed to give them help for doing nothing. Which is
the worst and what will the harvest be? (1955)

(19) Mr. Swift confined himself largely to an attack on the
"escalator system" of the Republican party which he said put a
man into the Senate, made him president of that body, the
Lieutenant-Governor, Governor, and finally United States Senator. He referred to Gaspar G. Bacon, his opponent, as a product of this system. Mr. Swift attacked Bacon's record in the

Senate, declaring his opponent to have been consistently opposed to measures favored by organized labor. (1932)

(20) As president, Mr. Hoover had nothing to do with the coming of the present depression. What has he done to ease the matter? He has worked day and night and called to Washington financiers, industrialists and bankers to consult with him. He has confronted this difficulty with great courage and as a result we did not go off the gold standard. (1932)

(21) The real issues in the Connecticut campaign which Senator Hiram Bingham is trying to hide are these: Bingham is for beer and against bread for the starving. Conover is for bread first. (1932)

(22) Mayor Murphy's statement asserted: "Probably no public official has had to contend with a worse brand of 'political rats' than myself. They seem to delight in spreading lies, rumors and propaganda, but it does not bother me as long as my conscience is clear and I know that I have never harmed any man intentionally. I love the thrill of combat and I want to remind my enemies that a good 'Irish terrier' can kill off any 'rat' in existence. . . ." Mayor Murphy categorically denied Whiteside's charges concerning the Somerville police station site, the number of Murphy relatives on the city payroll or his ownership of a mansion in Belmont, and asserted that Whiteside's "only interest in the taxpayer's movement is that of tax agitator so that he can scare up clients and collect more fees from them." (1932)

(23)   THREE MEN ON AN ISLAND

What Happens When Two of Them Stop Working Hard.

The United States is a representative democracy, that is, the public is represented directly in the Congress and indirectly in the executive branch, subject to the permissions and limitations of the Constitution as interpreted by the judicial branch, whose members are selected by the President with the approval of the Senate.

The sole purpose of our government is to insure us equal

opportunity to work, to provide us with safe money, to protect us from outside countries and to protect for each of us our saved property or money.

We are like three men on an island. Two of us work and divide up with the third man, who acts as the policeman and government. If two of them act as policemen, and by right of might, or authority of government, take most of what the remaining worker produces, we have a picture of our present plight. Ours is even worse because we have borrowed on what the third man has saved, and can only repay it by taking still more of what he earns. Still worse, because the two policemen juggle the money value so the third man no longer gets what he thinks he gets for his daily work. They tell him it's all for his own good, but just the same it enables them to snip off an extra slice for themselves of what he produces under cover of some phrase of plausible explanation.

Presently he stands up and looks around. He sees the other two are tremendously busy. But not doing hard work. They are mostly busy with complicated maneuvering of the things he has produced. And he sees they get more out of it themselves than they allow him to keep. So he stops working, too, and decides to join the other two in managing and policing things.

Then the whole thing breaks down. Everybody has to go to work, policemen and all. Of course, eventually there have to be policemen. But for a while at least the juiciest steak goes to the fellow who produces things, and the greatest honor goes to the fellow who saves of what he produces, so that in bad times all may eat and live. That is the next step here. (1938)

(24) Is Civilization Sinking Under the Dead Weight of Government? To the Editor of the *Sun*—Sir: Civilization is about through its advance. We are now beginning the dip which will be shorter than before, probably not over 300 years.

What a pity we cannot check and skip it! But that is impossible. It took many decades to develop money. But we have not advanced fast enough to comprehend and hold onto the fruits of our accomplishments. So we are breaking down money as a safe representative of saving. We must go all the way back to saving "things." Government has grown upon us until it absorbs probably a third of our earnings. Instead of being simply a cooperative device to preserve equal right, opportunity and protection, it asserts original jurisdiction over the conduct of life and industry. It has to fail because there is no such wisdom.

Organizations, of which labor unions are the outstanding example, have arisen and taken legislative powers that do not respond to the principles of democratic control. They exist in a democracy, but are not themselves democratic. We have no governmental power to control them. Our political parties and their representatives in office and out dare not openly oppose them, though a majority unorganized are out of sympathy with them.

Civilization is sinking. The "with-outs" are bound to dominate the "withs." When the accumulated savings of a hundred generations are used up, we must still go down, and tremble a long while at the bottom, before we turn again to saving, by preference or compulsion, under democracy or absolutism.

Au revoir, civilization! (1938)

(25) "GASOLINE" NEEDED

The President is merely going to run down the battery still more in endeavoring to start the car of state by spending further billions. It cannot be started without the gasoline of public confidence.

Some people may be fooled by the sound of the starter, but it will not take us to prosperity. (1938)

(26) LEGAL LOTTERY IS ON HIS LITTLE LIST

To the Editor of *New York Post:*

Sir: The Eighth Constitutional Convention is now in session at Albany. Come on, all you lottery-ticket buyers, send a postcard to Mr. Irwin Steingut, who is going to propose a State lottery for relief financing.

If we all send a telegram, letter or a postcard, it will put it over.

Gambling laws are like prohibition—a farce. (1938)

(27) Legion officials report that "several thousand" letters have been received endorsing the McNaboe-Devany Bill to exclude Communists from the Civil Service in this State.

Adjutant Stember comments:

"Nearly all the letters were from men and women who said they had written or telegraphed Governor Herbert H. Lehman to sign the bill. I imagine he must be deluged with such requests by now."

There should be no doubt that the overwhelming vote of the Legislature on the bill expressed an overwhelming public opinion that, as Adjutant Stember says:

"There is no reason why taxpayers should pay salaries of those who are openly or covertly plotting to overthrow the American Government."

It is, of course, exceedingly important that patriotic citizens should record their views with the Governor.

The element which is opposed to the McNaboe-Devany Bill is doing just that—and thereby providing final proof that the bill is needed.

For the propaganda drive against the bill is Communist-led and, in fact, was COMMUNIST-ORDERED.

The Daily Worker, organ of the Comintern, is publishing daily instructions to the "comrades" to "immediately wire Governor Lehman in Albany urging him to veto the bill."

And, as usual, the Communist sympathizers are living right up with the Reds.

For example, Teachers Union No. 5 is holding a mass meeting tonight which will "act" on the McNaboe-Devany Bill.

This Union has been OFFICIALLY BRANDED by the American Federation of Labor for its Communist control and Communist activities.

One of the speakers at its mass meeting will be Jerome Davis, ousted from the Yale Faculty for extreme radicalism, who will appear as President of the American Federation of Teachers. (1938)

INDEX

Ad hominem argument, 196
Alliteration, 82
Alice in Wonderland, 13, 47, 55, 56, 80
Alphabet, 51, 52
Ambiguity, 13, 14, 206ff, 208
Analogy, 77, 203, 204
Anaximines, 184
Anglo-Saxon (Old English), 71, 78, 84, 88, 91
Animal sounds, 53ff
Appeal to authority, 198, 199
Appeal to force, 199
Appeal to ignorance, 202
Appeal to pity, 198
Appeal to the people, 197ff
Argument, 114ff, 116
Aristotle, 22ff, 145
Articles, 79
Association, 114
Attitude, 73
Augustine, St., 139
Auxiliaries, 79

Bacon, Francis, 9, 23ff.
Begging the question, 201
Beneviste, Emile, 60
Beria, Lavrenti P., 180
Boethius, 144
Boswell, James, 105
Browne, Thomas, 105

Carlyle, Thomas, 210
Carnegie, Dale, 143
Carroll, Lewis, 13, 47, 55, 56, 80, 84
Charge of the Light Brigade, 43
Chaucer, Jeoffrey, 83, 90
Chinese ideographic writing, 53
Churchill, Winston, 15, 105, 205, 206
Circular reasoning, 201

Clemens, Samuel, 44ff, 46, 59, 76, 105, 175, 186, 204
Communism, 44
Complex question, 208
Conclusion, 115, 116
Conjunctions, 79
Conrad, Joseph, 105
Copernicus, 165, 182

Darwin, Charles, 185
Daydreaming, 5, 6
Deductive logic, 110ff
Definitory generalization, 169
Description, 114, 115
Dewey, John, 3, 33ff
Dickens, Charles, 75, 76
Dingle, Herbert, 105
Distribution, rules of, 124ff
Doctor Faustus, 59, 60
Donne, John, 105
Dostoyevsky, Feodor, 139, 147

Eddington, A. S., 105
Einstein, Albert, 3, 4, 170, 179, 181
Eisenhower, Dwight D., 84
Ellis, Havelock, 105
Emerson, Ralph Waldo, 105
Emotional argument, 196
Emotive generalization, 166
Empedocles, 184
Enthymeme, 135
Enumerative generalization, 171
Equivocation, 206ff
Eristratus, 184
Escapism, 5ff
Etymology, 71
Experience, 9
Eyewitnesses, 7

Faulty generalization, 200
Fielding, Henry, 124
Flaubert, Gustave, 12
Formal change, 77, 78, 80

Fowler, H. W., 175
Franklin, B., 208
Freud, S., 185
Frisch, Karl, 185
Function words, 77, 79

Galen, 184
Generalization, 165ff
Genetic fallacy, 197
Germanic consonant shift, 87, 88
Gibbon, E., 124
Goldberger, J., 178, 179
Grimm, J., 87

Harding, W. G., 84
Hardy, Thomas, 105
Hebrew, 85
Heffner, R. M. S., 49
Heraclitus, 105
Hercules, 42, 56
Herodotus, 211
Historical drift, 84
Hitler, Adolf, 7, 12, 210
Houdini, Harry, 8
Huckleberry Finn, 46
Hume, David, 105
Hypostatization, 206ff
Hypothesis, 177ff
Hypothetical generalizations, 177ff

Ibsen, Henrik, 203
Idols, Bacon's, 9ff
Imagery, 75, 76
Imperfect analogy, 203
Indo-European, 71, 73, 86, 87, 88
Inductive leap, 171, 172
Iron Curtain, 15
Irrelevance, 203

Jabberwocky, 55, 76, 80
James, William, 105
Joad, C. E. M., 144
Joseph, H. W. B., 146
Joyce, James, 120

Karok Indians, 11
Keats, John, 175

Lanfrey, P., 119
Language history, 82ff
Language as a creation of human
    society, 45ff
Language as a means of communi-
    cation, 43ff
Lapses, 84
Latin, 85, 88, 91
Leverrier, U. J. J., 181
Lexicography, 71
Lieber, L., 57
Leibniz, G., 146
Logical statements, 120ff
Longfellow, Henry Wadsworth, 119
Lucian, 42

Macaulay, Thomas Babbington, 210
Machiavelli, N., 119
Marlowe, Christopher, 59
Marx, Karl, 145
Marxism, 180
McManus, R., 99
Meaning, 71ff
Mencken, H. L., 12
Metaphor, 15, 16, 73, 75, 76, 204,
    205, 206
Middle English, 71, 83
Middle term, 126
Mill, John Stuart, 74, 76, 144, 146
Milton, J., 74, 75, 82, 105
Misuse of language, 10ff
Modern English, 55, 78, 79, 80, 84
Mussolini, Benito, 145

Napoleon Bonaparte, 176
Neutral language, 73, 75
Newton, Isaac, 3, 4, 170, 179
Nietzche, Friedrich Wilhelm, 120
Norman Conquest, 90
Nouns, 79, 80

Oakeshott, M., 145
Obstacles to thinking, 5
Order, 77
Orwell, G., 208

Padding, 118
Particular Affirmative, 121, 122
Particular Negative, 121, 122
Pasteur, Louis, 177
Pater, Walter, 105
Peck, H. T., 175
Peirce, C. S., 105
Persuasion, 75
Phonemes, 49, 52, 54, 55
Pitch, 79
Plato, 5, 17ff, 163
Poe, Edgar Allen, 187ff
Popular generalizations, 167
Post hoc ergo propter hoc fallacy, 201
Prejudice, 9, 10
Premises, 116
Propositions, 79
Probability, 173
Ptolemy, 165, 182

Rask, R. C., 87
"Real" names, 44
Reliable generalizations, 169ff
Rice, C. D., 57
Rules of distribution, 124ff
Ruskin, John, 105, 210

Sanskrit, 85
Sartre, Jean-Paul, 146
Scandinavian borrowings, 90
Scientific generalizations, 170
Seeing is believing, 7ff
Semantic ambiguity, 206ff
Semantic meaning, 70, 76
Shakespeare, 120, 147, 209, 212
"Social" names, 44
Sorites, 136ff
Special pleading, 202
Spengler, Oswald, 203
Stalin, Joseph, 145
Statistical enumerative generalization, 172

Sterne, Laurence, 144
Stevenson, Robert Louis, 105
Stewart, G. R., 105
Stress, 79
Subjective generalizations, 167
Swift, Jonathan, 210
Syntactic ambiguity, 208
Syntactic meaning, 70, 77ff
System of diagrams, 147ff
Sturtevant, E. H., 12
Syllogism, 125ff

Tabloids, 200
Taboo words, 11
Thinking, 3, 4, 5, 9
Thomas, St., 144
Thoreau, Henry David, 119, 210
Thucydides, 199, 200
Tolstoy, L., 119
Translation of sentences, 133
Trietschke, H., 145
Tyndall, J., 176

United Nations, 111ff, 121ff
Universal affirmative, 121, 122
Universal negative, 121, 122
Uniform enumerative generalization, 171ff
Unreliable generalizations, 166ff

Validity, 115ff
Verifiability, 180, 181
Verbs, 79, 80
Viking invasions, 90
Vocal organs, 49

Walter Mitty, 6
Webster's New World Dictionary, 71
Whorf, B. L., 55, 61ff
Winchell, Walter, 84

A NOTE ON THE TYPE

This book was set on the Linotype in ELECTRA, *designed by* W. A. Dwiggins. *The Electra face is a simple and readable type suitable for printing books by present-day processes. It is not based on any historical model, and hence does not echo any particular time or fashion. It is without eccentricities to catch the eye and interfere with reading—in general, its aim is to perform the function of a good book printing-type: to be read, and not seen.*

The book was composed, printed, and bound by H. WOLFF, *New York. Paper manufactured by* P. H. GLATFELTER COMPANY, *Spring Grove, Pennsylvania.*